hagst...
Brooklyn
ATLAS

In celebration of the Millennium

Stephan Van Dam presents the first

innovation in urban cartography in 50 years:

"...A sophisticated resource..." **NEW YORK TIMES**

"The best innovation in map design since the

globe was flattened onto paper!" **DIVERSION**

...For savvy travelers..." **PLAYBOY**

Brooklyn Atlas

While the area of today's Brooklyn had been home to the Canarsie Indians for millenia, it was first settled by the Dutch in 1635.

A metropolis in its own right, the City of Brooklyn joined the Bronx, Manhattan, Queens and Staten Island in 1898 to create the City of New York.

For the first time Brooklyn Atlas organizes the borough into three easily accessible parts:

...ps are shown in driving scale with each page 2 miles square, except for Downtown where a page equals 1 mile square.

THE BASICS

page **200**

Neighborhoods and streets are listed alphabetically and are easily found by page and grid coordinates (e.g. 201A)

SAMPLER

page **300**

Find attractions, banks, business, dining, entertainment, education, government, healthcare, kids' stuff, lodging, shopping, sports and recreation.

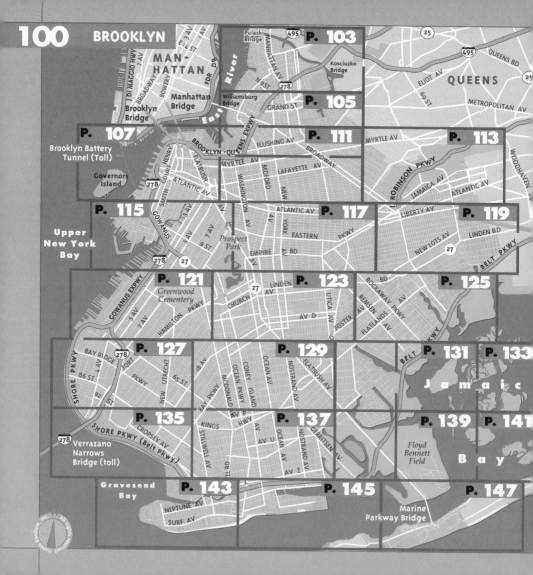

MAN-HATTAN

Pulaski Bridge

495 **P. 103**

Kosciuzko Bridge

QUEENS

25

495 QUEENS BD

ELIOT AV

68 ST

METROPOLITAN AV

Manhattan Bridge

Manhattan Bridge

Williamsburg Bridge

GRAND ST **P. 105**

East River

Brooklyn Bridge

FDR DR

I DI MAGGIO HWY

3 AV
E 14 ST
BROADWAY
BOWERY

4 AV

N 9 ST

278

FLUSHING AV **P. 111**

MYRTLE AV **P. 113**

WOODHAVEN

P. 107
Brooklyn Battery Tunnel (Toll)

BROOKLYN-QUEENS EXPWY

FLATBUSH

COURT

HENRY

SMITH

ATLANTIC AV

MYRTLE AV

LAFAYETTE

WASHINGTON AV

BEDFORD

NEW

BROADWAY

ROBINSON PKWY

JAMAICA AV

ATLANTIC AV

Governors Island

278

P. 115

3 AV

GOWANUS

5 AV

7 AV

9 ST

ATLANTIC AV **P. 117**

YORK

EASTERN PKWY

LIBERTY AV **P. 119**

LINDEN BD

Upper New York Bay

278 27

Prospect Park

EMPIRE AV BD

NEW LOTS AV

27

BELT PKWY

P. 121
Greenwood Cementery

LINDEN AV **P. 123**

P. 125

GOWANUS EXPWY

5 AV

7 AV

HAMILTON PKWY

CHURCH

27

AV D

UTICA AV

FOSTER

ROCKAWAY PKWY

REMSEN AV

FLATLANDS AV

BD

P. 127

BAY RIDGE

278

86 ST

92 ST

FORT

PKWY

NEW UTRECHT

65 ST

18 AV

MCDONALD

OCEAN PKWY

BAY PKWY

CONEY ISLAND

OCEAN AV

NOSTRAND AV

FLATBUSH AV

P. 129

BELT **P. 131** **P. 133**

Jamaic

SHORE PKWY

P. 135

CROPSEY AV

KINGS

STILLWELL AV

L RD

AV P

HWY

AV U

OCEAN AV

NOSTRAND AV

GERRITSEN AV

P. 137

AV Z

P. 139 **P. 141**

Floyd Bennett Field

Bay

278
Verrazano Narrows Bridge (toll)

SHORE PKWY (Belt Pkwy)

Gravesend Bay

P. 143

NEPTUNE AV

SURF AV

P. 145

Marine Parkway Bridge

P. 147

Brooklyn's Best

Brooklyn, NYC's most populous borough, is a metropolis in its own right, and home to 2.5 million people. It has been a cultural mecca, shipping capital, ocean front resort, and the gateway to America. One could fit four Manhattans into its 75 sq miles of land.

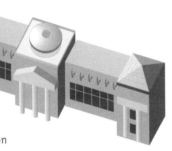

One out of every six Americans hails from what would still be the country's fourth largest city if it wasn't for the mistake: the annexation by New York City in 1898.

McKim Mead & White

Brooklyn Museum of Art

The museum's permanent collection includes paintings and sculpture by Rodin, Mondigliani, Degas, Monet, Chagall, Gaugin, Sargent, Bierstadt, plus one of the foremost collections of Egyptian art. 200 Eastern Pkwy, 718-638-5000. **116A**

Peter Luger

Candle-lit antebellum atmosphere, and the best steaks around. Cash only. Reservations are essential. 178 Broadway at Driggs Av, 718-387-7400. **104A**

Grand Army Plaza

America's leading landscape architects, Frederic Law Olmstead & Calvert Vaux, created the plaza in 1870. John Duncan designed the arch in honor of the Union Army. **116B**

River Café This haute dining barge boasts the most fabulous views of Manhattan and competes with the best food palaces anywhere. Reserve. 1 Water St, 718-522-5200. **107A**

Botanic Garden

Fifty acres of flora plus the largest public rose and bonsai collections in the country. 1000 Washington Av, 718-622-4433. **116C**

BAM The mecca of avant-garde performing arts scene is an annual rite and de rigueur for New Yorkers in the mix. The careers of composer Philip Glass, multimedia artist Laurie Anderson and choreographers Mark Morris and Bill T. Jones were launched here under the auspices of BAM's Next Wave Festival. Brooklyn Academy of Music 30 Lafayette St, 718-636-4100. **107D**

John H. Duncan

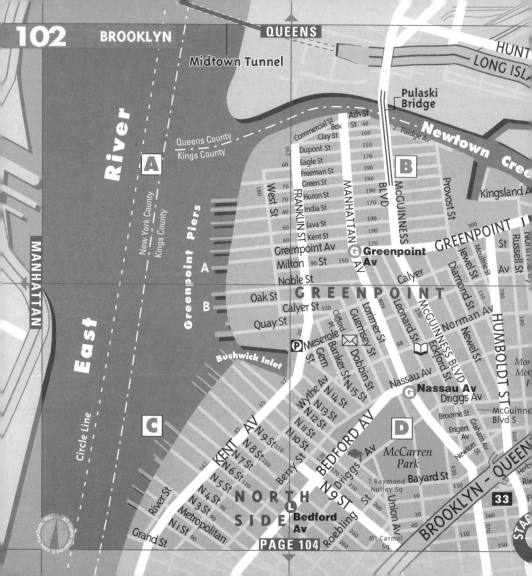

BROOKLYN

QUEENS

Midtown Tunnel

HUNT

LONG ISL

Pulaski Bridge

River

Newtown Cree

Ash St

Commercial St   Box   St 40

Clay St   100

Dupont St   150

Queens County   Eagle St   170

Kings County   Freeman St   190

2 Paidge Av

GREENPOINT I

B

60   Green St   190

Kingsland A

180   70   Huron St   190

Provost St

70   India St   170

Moultrie St

Java St   190

St

60   Kent St   190

Russell St

Jewel St

40

60   Greenpoint Av   170

Av

Milton   90 St 150

G **Greenpoint Av**

Diamond St   110

780

Noble St

Calyer

Greenpoint Piers

A

Oak St

G R E E N P O I N T

Leonard St   230

Norman Av

Newel St

B

Calyer St 120

809

McGuinness Av

HUMBOLDT ST

540

Quay St

Guernsey St

Eckford St

Clifford Pl   20

P Meserole

Bushwick Inlet

St   Gem

✉ Banker St N 15 St

Dobbin St

88

📖

Mor
McG
F

Nassau Av

G **Nassau Av**

Wythe Av   N 14 St

Driggs Av

N 13 St

McGuinne
Blvd S

N 12 St

Broome St

55

N II St

Engert
Av

C

N 10 St

Newton St

Graham St

KENT   85

N 9 St 110

Berry St

120

BEDFORD AV

D

McCarren Park

N 8 St 110

Av

141   N 7 St

170 210

Driggs

Bayard St

430

N 6 St 110

T Raymond
Nutley Sq

10

110

River St

N 5 St 90

BROOKLYN - QUEEN

N O R T H

N 4 St 90

N 9 ST

20

160 370

N 3 St 90

Union Av   260

40

Metropolitan

S I D E

L

Bedford Av

Roebling   240

33

N I St 90

Mt Carmel
Sq

110

150

Grand St

PAGE 104

MANHATTAN

East

Circle Line

FRANKLIN ST

West St

MANHATTAN AV

BLVD

McGUINNESS

Lorimer St

Bedford

START

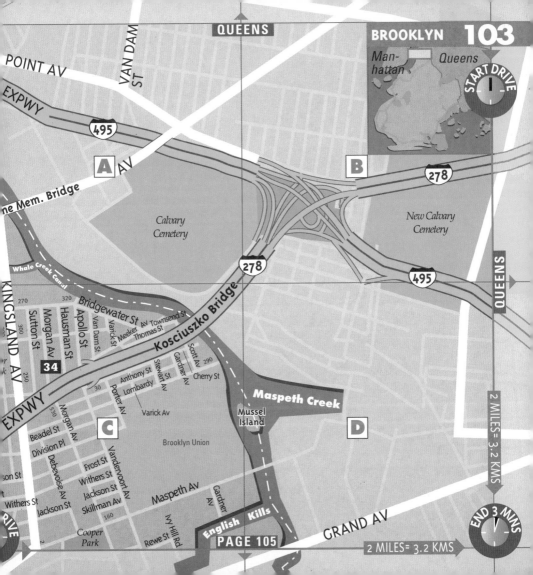

Man-hattan   Queens

START DRIVE

POINT AV

EXPWY

495

VAN DAM ST

A AV

ne Mem. Bridge

B

278

Calvary
Cemetery

New Calvary
Cemetery

QUEENS

Whale Creek Canal

KINGSLAND AV

278

495

270
320
Bridgewater St
Morgan Av
Hausman St
Apollo St
Sutton St
300
250
Van Dam St
Varick St
Meeker AV
Thomas St
Townsend St

34

Kosciuszko Bridge

Scott Av
290

EXPWY

30
Anthony St
Lombardy
Porter Av
Stewart Av
Gardner Av
Cherry St

Varick Av

C

Maspeth Creek

Mussel
Island

D

530
Morgan Av
Beadel St
Division Pl
Debevoise Av
Brooklyn Union

Frost St
Withers St
Jackson St
Skillman Av
160
Vandervoort Av

son St
Withers St
Jackson St

Maspeth Av

Gardner AV

English Kills

PAGE 105

GRAND AV

Cooper
Park

Ivy Hill Rd
Rewe St

RIVE

2 MILES = 3.2 KMS

2 MILES = 3.2 KMS

END 3 MINS

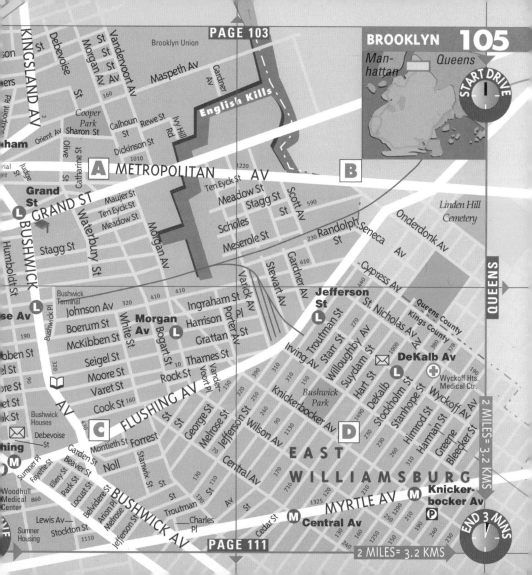

Bargemusic
Old Ful

F U L T O N

F E R R Y

Liberty & Ellis
Island Ferries

*Battery
Park*

A

Governors
Island
Ferry

B

2

East River

Brooklyn
Heights
Promenade

3

4

5

B R O O K L Y N

Staten
Island
Ferry

H E I G H T S

New York County
Kings County

6

Brooklyn He

Montague

Furman St

Columbia Pl

Willow Pl

7

27

278

Carder Rd

Castle
Williams

**Governors
Island**

Wheeler Av

Hay Rd

Early Bird Rd

Fort Jay

C O L U M B I A

Long Island
College Hospital

Hi

A

8

Craig Rd N

Gresham Rd

C

Division Rd

S T R E E T

W A T E R

9A

60

Warren St

440

Columbia St

Baltic St

Co
Ve

Enright Rd

F R O N T

Kane St

Tiffany Pl

Irving St

Cheever Pl

Warren
Pl

Craig Rd S

Yankee
Pier

Brooklyn
Battery
Tunnel
(Toll)

D

9B

Sedgwick St

50

Degraw St

VAN BRUNT ST

Sackett St

Hicks St

BQE

HENRY ST

Strong Pl

Tango
Pier

Ferry Pl

Hamilton Av

Union St

P

490

Lima
Pier

Buttermilk Channel

10

President St

Carroll St

150

220

220

Summit St

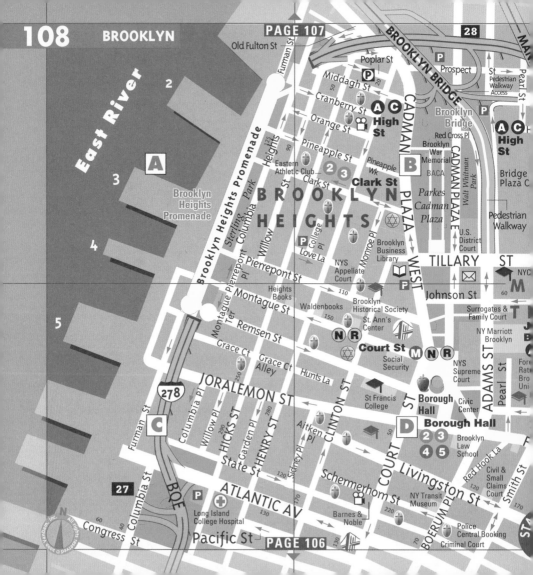

PAGE 107
PAGE 106

28

East River

A

2

3

4

5

Old Fulton St
Furman St

Poplar St
Prospect

BROOKLYN BRIDGE

MAIN

P

St
Pedestrian
Walkway
Access

Pearl St

Middagh St

Cranberry St

Orange St

A C High St

Pineapple St

Brooklyn Heights Promenade

Columbia Park

Sterling Pl

Willow St

Heights St

Eastern
Athletic Club

Pineapple Wk

Clark St

2 3

Clark St

Brooklyn
Bridge

Red Cross Pl
Brooklyn
War
Memorial

BACA

B

A C High St

Bridge
Plaza C

Brooklyn
Heights
Promenade

B R O O K L Y N

H E I G H T S

College Pl

P

Love La

Monroe Pl

NYS
Appellate
Court

Brooklyn
Business
Library

Parkes
Cadman
Plaza

CADMAN PLAZA WEST

CADMAN PLAZA

Walt Whitman
Park

U.S.
District
Court

Pedestrian
Walkway

Brooklyn
Heights
Promenade

Pierrepont Pl

Pierrepont St

Montague Ter

Montague St

Heights
Books

110

Waldenbooks

150

Brooklyn
Historical Society

St. Ann's
Center

TILLARY ST

Johnson St

60

NYC M

Remsen St

Grace Ct

Grace Ct
Alley

Hunts La

N R

Court St

Social
Security

M N R

Surrogates &
Family Court

NY Marriott
Brooklyn

NYS
Supreme
Court

T

ADAMS ST

Pearl St

Fore
Rat
Bro
Uni

278

JORALEMON ST

Columbia Pl

Willow Pl

250

290

Garden Pl

HICKS ST

HENRY ST

280

Aitken Pl

Sidney Pl

CLINTON ST

St Francis
College

D

Borough
Hall

Borough Hall

2 3
4 5

Civic
Center

Brooklyn
Law
School

Furman St

BQE

27

Columbia St

State St

120

Schermerhorn St

COURT ST

Livingston St

120

Red Hook La

Civil &
Small
Claims
Court

Smith St

170

P

Long Island
College Hospital

ATLANTIC AV

130

Barnes &
Noble

NY Transit
Museum

220

BOERUM ST

70

Police
Central Booking
Criminal Court

STA

N

60

40

Congress St

Pacific St

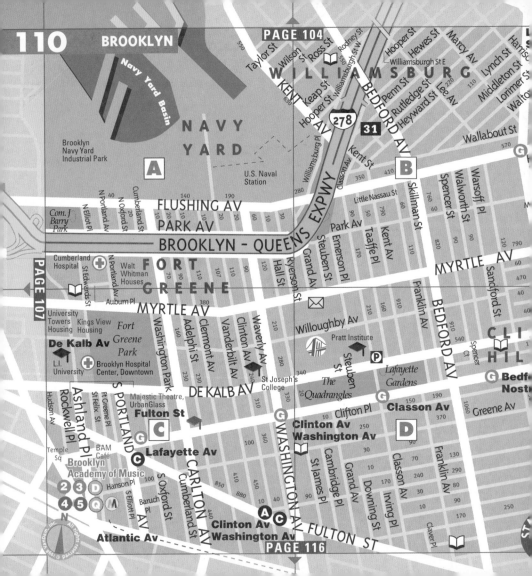

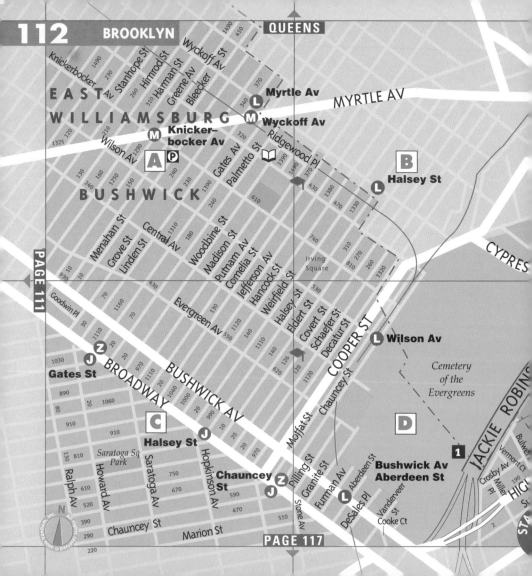

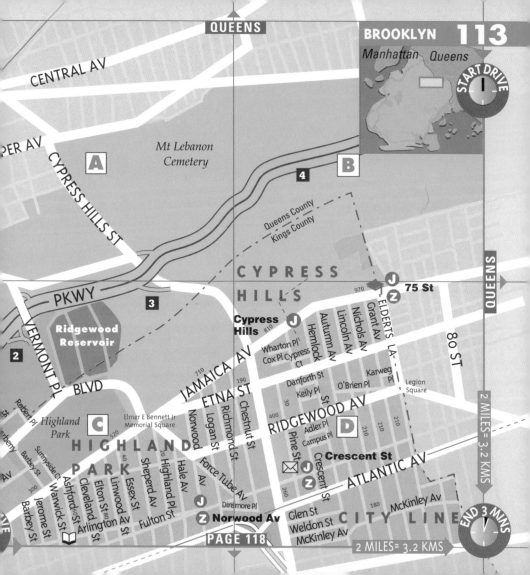

Buttermilk Channel

10
12
Atlantic Basin

PAGE 106

Summit St
Carroll St
278
26

220
150
120
560

HENRY ST
1 Pl
Woodhull St
2 Pl
3 Pl
Rapelye St
4 Pl
Luquer St

CLINTON ST
240
210
70

COURT ST
70
430

Douglass St
Smith St
Smith St
Sackett St
Union St
President St

Baisley House

Carroll St
F G

C A R R O L L
G A R D E N S

Bowne St
Seabring St
Coles
Toll
Plaza

Commerce St

Pioneer St
King St
Sullivan St

210
20

Imlay St

VAN BRUNT ST

Delavan St
Verona St

140

Huntington St

B

SMITH ST

Nelson St
5 St
4 St
3 St

Dermet Pl

Ferris St
Coffey St
Wolcott St

Dikeman St

Richards St
Dwight St
Visitation Pl

Red Hook Park

Columbia St

W 9 St
60

Mill St

St
St

**R E D
H O O K**

39
41
44
46

Conover St
Reed St

Van Dyke St
Beard St

20

Creamer St

Hicks

Lorraine St

Henry

Clinton St

Bush St
Centre St

St

GOWANUS

**Smith St
9 St**
F G

Canal

6 St Basin
7 St Basin

Garnet St

9 ST

Sigourney St

Halleck St

Otsego St

20

Henry St Basin

Bay St

Halleck St

Court St

Bryant St

Percival St

St

COURT ST

660

St

St

Gowanus

Hamilton Pl

Hamilton

D

1

2A

Breakwater Terminal

Erie Basin
C

Columbia St

Port Auth Grain Terminal

2

20 St
21 St
23 St

23

EXPWY

M
N
R

2B

29 St
30 St
31 St
33 St
35 St

Gowanus Bay

278

PAGE 120

200
210
680

18 St
19 St
20 St
21 St
22 St
23 St

ST

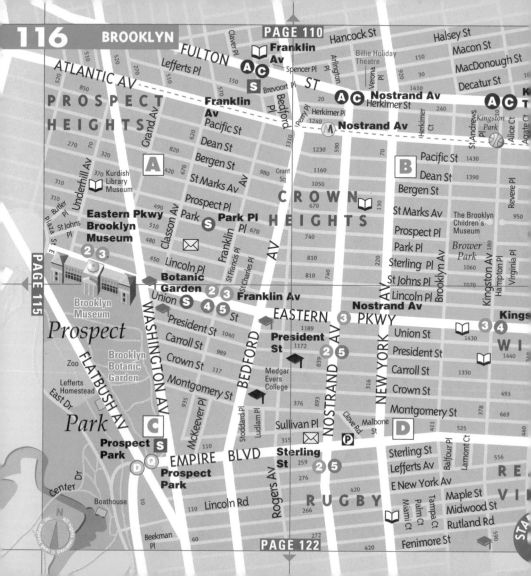

PAGE 110
PAGE 115
PAGE 122

PROSPECT HEIGHTS

CROWN HEIGHTS

Prospect Park

Brooklyn Museum

Brooklyn Botanic Garden

RUGBY

ATLANTIC AV

FULTON ST

Franklin Av

Nostrand Av

Lefferts Pl

Spencer Pl

Hancock St

Halsey St

Macon St

MacDonough St

Decatur St

Billie Holiday Theatre

Herkimer St

Herkimer Pl

Pacific St

Dean St

Bergen St

St Marks Av

Prospect Pl

Park Pl

Lincoln Pl

Franklin Av

Union St

President St

Carroll St

Crown St

Montgomery St

Sullivan Pl

EMPIRE BLVD

Sterling St

Lefferts Av

E New York Av

Maple St

Midwood St

Rutland Rd

Fenimore St

Lincoln Rd

Beekman Pl

Kurdish Library Museum

Eastern Pkwy Brooklyn Museum

Botanic Garden

EASTERN PKWY

Nostrand Av

President St

Medgar Evers College

Prospect Park

Brower Park

The Brooklyn Children's Museum

Kingston Park

Prospect Park Zoo

Lefferts Homestead

Boathouse

Underhill Av

Grand Av

Classon Av

Washington Av

Flatbush Av

Bedford Av

Franklin Av

Rogers Av

Nostrand Av

New York Av

Kingston Av

Brooklyn Av

WI

RE

VI

Lewis Av
MALCOM X BLVD
Chauncey St
Saratoga St
Ralph Av
Marion St
Sumpter St
McDougal
ny Av
Bainbridge St
Brevoort Housing

Fulton Chauncey
Park
Marion St

A C FULTON ST **A C** ✉

Utica Av
Jewell McKoy La
Harmony Park

O C E A N H I L L

Ralph Av

Hunterfly Pl
Suydam Pl
Kane Pl
Columbus Pl
Prescott Pl
Bancroft Pl
Dewey Pl
Louis Pl
Roosevelt Pl

A T L A N T I C A V **B**

rkimer St
Hattie Jones Ct
erfaith spital and dical Center

A

W E E K S V I L L E

Kingsborough Housing

B R O W N S V I L L E

Troy Av
St Johns Park

P

St Mary's Hospital

Schenectady Av
Utica Av
Rochester Av
Buffalo Av
Ralph Av
Howard Av
Saratoga Av
Hopkinson Av
Rockaway Av

YORK AV
PKWY

P

Howard Housing

✉

ASTERN PKWY **3 4** Utica Av

A T E

EASTERN
EAST NEW

Lincoln Terrace Park

Portal St
Union St

KINGS

Grafton St
Tapscott St
Union St
Legion St
Saratoga Av
Strauss St
Herzl St
Amboy St
Bristol St
Chester St
Thatford St
Rockaway Av

Pitkin Av

Sutter Av

Ford St

C

E A S T F L A T B U S H

Sutter Av
Rutland Rd **3**

3

Blake Square

Blake Av **D**

Dumont Av

MPIRE BLVD

EN

Saratoga Av **3**

Howard Gardens

Livonia Av
Hopkinson Av

AGE

Kingsbrook Jewish Medical Center

E 49 St
E 46 St
E 45 St

UTICA AV
REMSEN AV

Rutland Rd
Winthrop St
Clarkson Av

ROCK-AWAY PKWY

Lenox Rd

Howard Av

Riverdale Av

Newport St

END 3 MINS

2 MILES = 3.2 KMS

PAGE 118

PAGE 112

Cooke Ct

Sumpter St
MacDougal St
Broadway 310
Eastern Pkwy 40

Hull St
Rockaway Av Somers St

FULTON

Herkimer St

ATLANTIC

Radde Pl
Maroni Pl
Gunther Pl
Hopkinson

EASTERN PKWY

EAST NEW YORK AV

Monaco Pl

Pleasant Pl

A AV

Sherlock Pl

Stewart St
Conway St
Falchon Pl

Marginal St W
Marginal St E

Sunnyside Av
Miller

JAMAICA AV

Arlington Av

Fulton St

Van Siclen Av

ATLANTIC AV

LIBERTY AV

EXT

B R O A D W A Y

JCT

Truxton St

Sackman St
Jardine Pl
Havens Pl
Williams Pl

Jewell Square

A C **Broadway**
East New York

J **Alabama Av**

M **L**
Atlantic Av

A C
Liberty Av

B

Glenmore Av

Pitkin Av

Jerome St
Barbey St
Schenck Av
Warwick St

A C
Van Siclen Av

East NY Neighborhood
Family Care Center

GRANVILLE PAYNE AV

Sheffield Av
Georgia Av
Alabama Av
Williams Av
Hinsdale Av
Snediker Av
Van Sinderen Av

L **Sutter Av**

Van Siclen Av
Miller Av
Bradford St
Wyona St
Vermont St
New Jersey St

Hendrix St

Blake

Linton Park

E A S

Dum

3 **Van Sicle**
Av

3 **Pennsylvania Av**

Howard Housing

Gaston Blvd

Junius St
Powell St
Sackman St
Watkins St
Osborn St
Rockaway Av
Thatford Av
Christopher Av

P

PAGE 117

Pitkin Av
Herzl St
Amboy St

Chester St
Bristol St

Sutter Av

Blake Av

Dumont Av
Livonia Av

Saratoga Av
Strauss St

B R O W N S V I L L E

Newport St

Hopkinson Av

Brownsville

Brooklyn Heritage House

Housing

SJ Tilden Houses

Dyke

Housing

C **3**
Rockaway Av

Riverdale Av

Lott Av

Christopher Av
Sackman St
Watkins St
Osborn St
Thatford Av

3 **Junius St**

L **Livonia Av**

N E W
L O T S

D

PENNSYLVANIA AV

NEW LOTS AV

Van Siclen Av
Miller Av
Bradford St
Wyona St
Vermont St
New Jersey St
Sheffield Av
Alabama Av

Hendrix St
McClai

LINDEN BL

STA

L **New Lots**
Av

PAGE 124

N All rights

Z J **Norwood Av**

Weldon St
McKinley Av
Hill St
1030

C I T Y   L I N E

Manhattan   Queens

START DRIVE

Wells St

60

280
780

890
980

EUCLID AV

S Conduit Av

N Conduit Av

244

Atkins Av
Berriman St
Sheperd Av
Essex St
nwood St
nd St

170
170
190
130
460
60

Euclid Av

A C

Doscher St

380

Chestnut St
Crystal St
Fountain Av
Logan St
Milford St
Montauk Av

510

Pine St
Crescent St
Hemlock St

Lincoln Av
Sheridan Av

A **Grant
Av**

Grant Av
Elderts La

670

B

Drew St
Forbell St

Ruby St

Emerald St

Amber St
220

480

A C
Shepherd Av

Belmont Av

P

Sutter Av

Blake Av

Autumn Av

Pitkin Av
Subway
Yards

450

Dumont Av

Cypress
Hills
Housing

N E W   Y O R K

610
370
590

2650

L I N D E N   B L V D

Louis H Pink

910
680

Queens County
Kings County

QUEENS

3 **New Lots
Av**

710

Logan St
Milford St
Montauk Av
Atkins Av
Berriman St
Sheperd Av
Essex St
Linwood St
Elton Av
Cleveland St

790
480
790

Fountain Av

Euclid Av

Holly Av

Loring Av

Housing

Ashford St
Hegeman St
ck St

27

Stanley Av

Lincoln Av
Sheridan Av

D   Wortman Av

2 MILES = 3.2 KMS

C

610
580
980

Hemlock St

610

610

Cozine Av

Stanley Av

930

790

Boulevard

720

Housing

330

Wortman Av

Cozine Av

Flatlands Av

610

Old Mill Rd

620

610

Flatlands Av

157 Av

END 3 MINS

Schenck Av

890

270

DRIVE

820

PAGE 125

2 MILES= 3.2 KMS

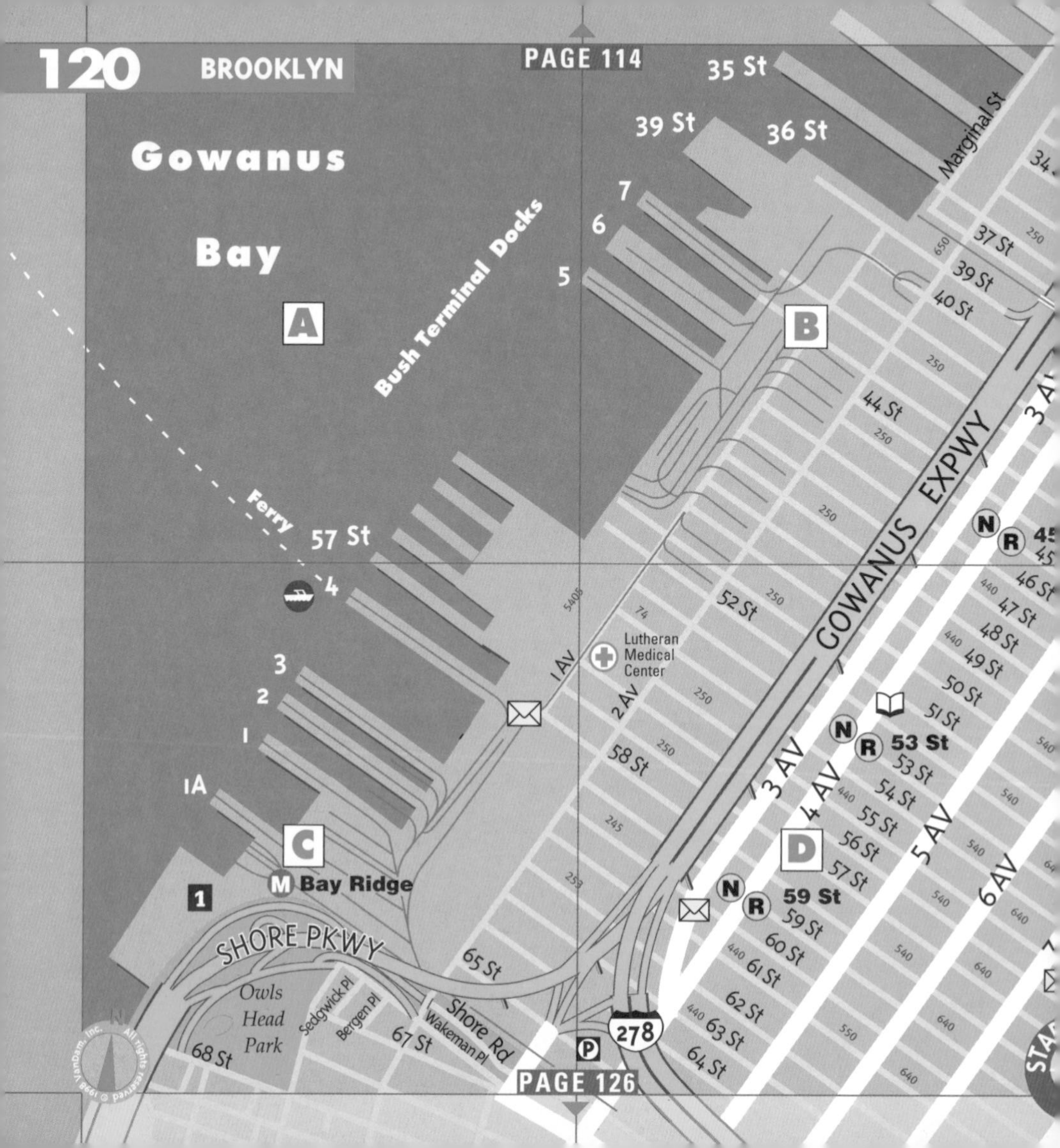

Gowanus

Bay

A

Bush Terminal Docks

35 St

39 St
36 St

Marginal St

34

37 St

39 St

40 St

7

6

5

B

44 St

Ferry

57 St

4

250

250

250

3 Av

Gowanus Expwy

N R 45
45

46 St

47 St

48 St

49 St

50 St

51 St

N R 53 St
53 St

54 St

55 St

56 St

57 St

N R 59 St
59 St

60 St

61 St

62 St

63 St

64 St

3

2

1

1A

1

M Bay Ridge

C

54

5405

74

1 AV

Lutheran
Medical
Center

2 AV

58 St

250

250

250

3 AV

4 AV

440

440

D

5 AV

6 AV

540

540

540

540

540

640

640

640

STA

SHORE PKWY

Owls
Head
Park

68 St

Sedgwick Pl

Bergen Pl

65 St

67 St

Shore Rd

Wakeman Pl

253

245

440

550

640

278

P

PAGE 126

Manhattan   Queens

START DRIVE I

25 St
M N R
24 St
25 St
26 St
27 St
28 St
29 St
30 St
31 St
32 St
33 St
P 200
200
200
820

B
N M
R
36 St
35 St
36 St
36 St

A

38 St
39 ST
5 AV
6 AV
7 AV
37 St
36 St

23 St
270
20 St
21 St
22 St
6 AV
320
330
7 AV

8 AV

B

Greenwood Cemetery

Terrace Pl
Seeley St
Vanderbilt St

MCDONALD AV

Greenwood Av

Fort Hamilton Pkwy
F

PAGE 122

CATON AV

E 4 St
E 3 St
E 2 St

Sunset Park
540

6 AV
640
7 AV
750
8 AV
830
9 AV
940

B M 9 Av
Hefferman Square

HAMILTON PKWY
Minna St
Michell Pl
Bills Pl
Chester Av
3301
St

I 2 Av
Tehama
Clara
Louisa
St
37 St
35 St
36 St
Story St
112

Albemarle Rd

310
310

CHURCH AV

1050
1050

C

740
760
830
750
750
860
830

Maimonides Medical Center
970

B M
Alben Memorial Square

9 Av
FORT

11 AV

D

1240
38 St
39 St
40 St
41 St
42 St
43 St
44 St
45 St
46 St
47 St
1250
1250
1250
1250
1250
1449

Church Av
Av C
110

F

1470
1440
1440

15 Av

Dahill Rd

KENSINGTON

Fort Hamilton Pkwy

12 Av
13 Av
14 Av

750
830
950
940
850

8 AV
9 AV

B M
50 St
1150

END 3 MINS

2 MILES = 3.2 KMS

278

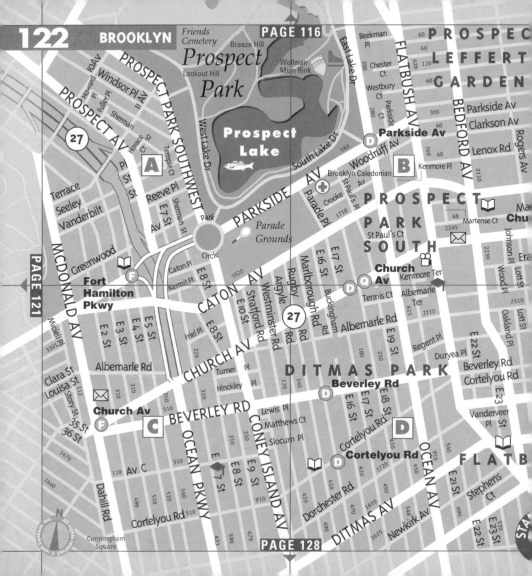

Friends Cemetery

Prospect Park

Breeze Hill
Lookout Hill
Wollman Mem Rink

Beekman Pl
Chester Ct
Westbury Ct
Parkside Ct

PROSPECT LEFFERT GARDEN

60
60
620
120
60
300
60

Parkside Av
Clarkson Av
769 60
Lenox Rd
Rogers Av

Prospect Lake

East Lake Dr
West Lake Dr

South Lake Dr

Woodruff Av

Parkside Av Ⓓ

FLATBUSH AV
BEDFORD AV

2110

Kenmore Pl Ⓑ

PROSPECT PARK SOUTH

48
Martense Ct
2245

Chu

Ma

PROSPECT PARK SOUTHWEST

Windsor Pl
Howard
Fuller Pl
Sherman

Horace St
Temple Ct
Sherman St

IOAV
PROSPECT AV

27

Terrace
Seeley
Vanderbilt

Reeve Pl

Pl
St
St

E 7 St

Caton Pl
Kermit Pl

Park
Circle

PARKSIDE

Parade Pl
Crooke
St Paul's Pl

Brooklyn Caledonian

1710

Parade Grounds

St Paul's Ct

E 17 St
E 16 St

Johnson Pl
Wood Pl

2230

Era

Church Av Ⓓ

Kenmore Ter

E 18 St

Albemarle Ter

2510

Lott St
Oakland Pl

Greenwood

Fort Hamilton Pkwy Ⓕ

1020

CATON AV

E 8 St
E 8 St

Friel Pl
220

Stratford Rd
Westminster Rd

Argyle Rd

Rugby Rd

Marlborough Rd

Buckingham Rd

27

Tennis Ct

Albemarle Rd

615
2110

Regent Pl
Duryea Pl

180
250

Beverley Rd
Cortelyou Rd

E 23

DITMAS PARK

E 19 St

E 22 St

McDONALD AV

Midell Pl
3301

E 2 St
E 3 St
E 4 St
E 5 St

Albemarle Rd

Clara St
Louisa St
Story St
35 St
36 St

112
310
310

Church Av Ⓕ

CHURCH AV

Tumer Pl
Hinckley

350
510

C **BEVERLEY RD**

Lewis Pl
Matthews Ct
Slocum Pl

1470

Dahill Rd

Av C

OCEAN PKWY

E 7 St
E 8 St

110

CONEY ISLAND AV

E 8 St
E 9 St

310
250

Beverley Rd Ⓓ

E 16 St
E 17 St
E 18 St

Cortelyou Rd

D

120
140

160

Cortelyou Rd Ⓓ

E 16 St

1720
410

Dorchester Rd

OCEAN AV

E 21 St

Stephens Ct

FLATB

910
450
490

1610
1615

490

540

Vanderveer Pl
E 23 St

E 22 St
E 23 St

1440

Cortelyou Rd

490
510
540
510

510

433
590
479

DITMAS AV

NewkirkAv

STA

1020

Cunningham Square

N
Vanguard Inc © All rights reserved

PAGE 121

Fenimore St
Hawthorne St
Winthrop St

5 **Winthrop St**

Kings County Hospital

Kingsbrook Jewish Medical Center

Kingsboro Psychiatric Center

Health Science Center SUNY Downstate

27

A **LINDEN BLVD** **B**

CHURCH AV

Raleigh Pl
Fairview Pl

E 31 St
E 32 St
E 34 St
E 35 St
Brooklyn Av
E 37 St
E 38 St
E 39 St
E 40 St
Albany Av
E 42 St
E 43 St
Troy Av
E 45 St
E 46 St
Schenectady Av
E 48 St
E 49 St
E 51 St
E 52 St
E 53 St
E 54 St
E 55 St

Snyder Av

E 58 St
E 59 St

UTICA AV

Tilden Av

E 56 St
E 57 St

P

NEW YORK AV

Holy Cross Cemetery

Beverly Rd

Beverley Rd
2 **5**

CLARENDON RD

F A R R A G U T

KINGS HWY

Ralph Av

2 MILES = 3.2 KMS

E 28 St
E 29 St

Newkirk Av **C**

AV D

D

Jodie Ct
Whitty La

Newkirk Av
Victor Rd

Brooklyn Av

E 37 St
E 38 St
E 39 St

Albany Av
E 40 St
E 42 St
E 43 St
Foster Av
E 45 St
Troy Av
E 46 St

2 **5**

Paerdegat Park

Harwood Pl

FOSTER AV

Farragut Pl
Brooklyn Rd

Rogers Av

Farragut Rd

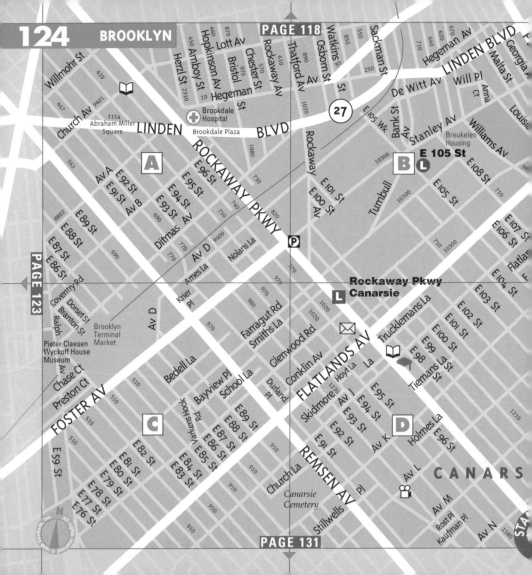

Manhattan Queens

START DRIVE

570

Jersey Av

VANIA AV

910

Wortman Houses

Linden Houses

Vermont St

Dale Pl

20

Vandalia

1260 Croton Loop

1270 Delmar Loop

Twin Pines Dr

650

1420 Freeport Loop

270

Wortman Av

898

Schenck Av

Cozine Av

Flatlands Av

1020

Vandalia Av

Ardsley Loop

A

Van Siclen Av

Bethel Loop

Elmira Loop

Schroeders Av

STARRETT CITY

1490 Homell Loop

870

1440 Geneva Loop

1180

800 Erskine

NYS Office of Mental Retardation and Developmental Disabilities

SPRING CREEK

Walker St

Elton St

St

Seaview Av

Seaview Loop

B

Seaview Av

11320

11320

Spring Creek Park (no access)

QUEENS

F4 St

F5 St

F6 St

1210

F7 St

F8 St

F9 St

F10 St

10310

1410

Seaview Av

1410

1530

Bayview Houses

C

Border Av

14

Fresh Creek Basin

BELT PKWY

D

North Channel

Elders Point Marsh

2 MILES = 3.2 KMS

END 3 MINS

Owls Head Park

PAGE 120

Shore Rd Dr

Sedgwick Pl
Bergen Pl
Wakeman Pl
67 St
Senator St

68 St
Bliss Ter
Louise Ter
70 St
Mackay Pl
Ridgecrest Ter
Perry Ter
Bay Cliff Ter
Madeline Ct
Bay
Ridge

62 St
63 St
64 St
66 St
67 ST
Leif Ericsson Park
68 St
Senator St

72 Ct
71 St
72 St
73 St
74 St
Bay Ridge Pl
24 Hr Rite-Aid

A

B   **Bay Ridge Av**

Old Glory Look Out

Ovington Av
Vista Pl
72 St
73 St
74 St

278

BAY RIDGE

Narrows Av
76 St
77 St
78 St

BAY RIDGE PKWY

Harbor View Ter
Colonial Ct
Harbor La
Westerly La

79 St
80 St
81 St
82 St
83 St

Colonial Rd
Ridge Blvd

84 St
85 St

77 St   **R**   76 St
77 St
78 St
79 St
80 St
81 St
82 St
83 St
84 St
85 St

McKinley Park

McDonald Square

W E Coffey Square

Comfort Inn Brooklyn

3 AV
4 AV
5 AV
6 AV
7 AV

GOWANUS EXPWY

SHORE PKWY

Shore Ct

86 St
87 St
88 St
89 St
90 St
91 St

Monastery Square

C

Colonial Gardens

FORT HAMILTON

Oliver St

Ridge
93 St
94 St
95 St
96 St

Hamilton Wk
Lafayette Wk

93 St
94 St
95 St
96 St

86 St
87 St
88 St
89 St
91 St
92 ST

86 St   **R**

Forest Pl

Gelston Av

D

Dyker Pl

FORT HAMILTON PKWY

Battery Av
Parrott Pl

10 AV
84 St
85 St
86 St

PAGE 134

Manhattan Queens

START DRIVE

640

750

8 Av

830

9 Av

940

10 Av

49 St

1120

50 St

640

740

850

940

1150

52 St

53 St

50 St

51 St

6120

720

850

940

1050

54 St

55 St

1220

7 AV

8 Av

870

920

Bocchino D
Memorial Plaza

1050

55 St

56 St

13 Av

B

720

A

1010

Fort
Hamilton Pkwy

1240

57 St

58 St

14 Av

15 Av

1440

1540

Leif
Ericsson
Square

FORT HAMILTON PKWY

62 St

63 St

6310

1010

1060

Tabor Ct

1220

59 St

60 St

61 St

1440

1540

1630

16 Av

17 Av

850

961

New
Utrecht Av

62 St

1540

P

950

1060

Regina
Opera

1250

64 St

N

B

M

1550

1750

940

1020

65 ST

66 St

67 St

1430

NEW UTRECHT AV

1640

1750

950

1050

Ovington Av

Bay Ridge Av

70 St

71 St

1750

Y RIDGE PKWY

1040

1250

72 St

73 St

74 St

1430

Duryea Ct

Ovington Ct

18 Av

N

1010

C

1250

1440

71 St

B

M

D

Wallaston Ct
Cameron Ct

1700

1250

76 St

77 St

78 St

79 St

80 St

1440

N E W   U T R E C H T

68 St

1250

81 St

82 St

83 St

1540

1650

1650

1760

1670

1750

END 3 MINS

2 MILES= 3.2 KMS

2 MILES= 3.2 KMS

PAGE 128

B YKER
E I G H T S

PAGE 123

PAGE 129

PAGE 138

Paerdegat Av S
Troy Pl
Glendale Ct
Glenwood Rd
Av H
Troy Av
E 45 St
E 43 St
E 42 St
Albany Av
Schenectady Av
E 46 St
E 48 St
E 49 St
E 51 St
E 52 St
E 53 St
E 54 St
E 55 St
E 56 St
E 57 St
E 58 St
E 59 St
Av I
Av J
Av K
Av L
Av M
Av N
Av O
Av S

KINGS HWY

A

FLATLANDS AV

Ryder Sq

Paerdegat Av S
Paerdegat Av N
South Shore Plaza

E 76 St
E 77 St
E 78 St
E 79 St
E 80 St
E 81 St
E 82 St
E 83 St
E 84 St
E 85 St
Av I
Av J
Av K

Paerdegat 2 St
Pdgt 3 St
Pdgt 4 St
Pdgt 5 St
Pdgt 6 St
Pdgt 7 St
Pdgt 8 St
Pdgt 9 St
Pdgt 10 St
Paerdegat Av N

B

Paerdegat

Canar Cemet

Bergen Av
E 73 St
E 72 St
M
Bergen Ct
Royce Pl
Royce St
Peri La

RALPH AV
UTICA AV
FLATLANDS

GEORGETOW

Av N
Av T
Av U
Av V

Charles W Boyce Square

Veterans Av
Mill La

E 66 St
E 67 St
E 68 St
E 63 St
E 64 St
E 65 St

E 71 St
E 72 St
E 73 St
E 69 St
E 70 St

D

Strickland Av
Mill Av

East Mill Ba

Ohio Wk

E
E 40 St
E 41 St
Lott Pl
Harden St
E 43 St
Father Kehoe Sq
Baughman Pl

Av P
Hendrickson St
Coleman St
Kimball St
Quentin Rd
Ryder St
E 38 St
E 37 St
Fillmore Av

C

Peter Trust Square

FLATBUSH AV

Fillmore Av
Av S

E 56 St
E 57 St
E 58 St
E 59 St
E 60 St
Pearson St

E 61 ST

E 60 Pl
Mayfair Dr N

N

Manhattan Queens

START DRIVE

Pl

Av L

E 93 St

E 94 St

E 95 St

E 96 St

1940

1540

wells Pl

E 91 St

Av M

Rost Pl

Kaufman Pl

Av N

1590

REMSEN AV

E 89 St

Canarsie

1520

1580

Bayview
Houses

E 88 St

Mathews E 92 St

Seaview Rd

Seaview Av

St Jude Pl

E 87 St

1520

AV

86 St

1520

Seaview Ct E 96 St

E 93 St

St

A E R D E G A T

A

E 92 St

Schenck

Skidmore

E 91 St

1410

13 St

1410

B

1410

14 St

Skidmore
Pl

Canarsie
Pier

15 St

Canarsie
Beach
Park

BELT PKWY

13

Sebago
Canoe Club

Basin

North Channel

PAGE 132

gen Av

St

2210

2210

Canarsie
Pol

2210

B E R G E N

C

D

2410

B E A C H

X

2410

Jamaica Bay
Riding Academy

2 MILES = 3.2 KMS

AV Y

2410

Nestepol
Marsh

END 3 MINS

2 MILES = 3.2 KMS

PAGE 125

14

ROCKAWAY PKWY

E 93 St
E 104 St
E 103 St
E 102 St
E 101 St
E 100 St
E 99 St
E 98 St
E 96 St
E 95 St
E 94 St
E 92 St
E 93 St
E 91 St
E 92 St

F 9 St
F 10 St

Av L
Av M
Av N

Rost Pl
Kaufman Pl
Mathews Pl

1940
1540
1580
1520
1520

A

Bayview Houses

BELT PKWY

Fresh Creek

O-O Basin

B

Canarsie Rd
Seaview Av
St Jude Pl
Seaview Av
Seaview Ct
Skidmore Pl
Schenck St
Av

Skidmore Pl

Canarsie Beach Park

13

Canarsie Pier

Channel

Gateway Nat

North

C

D

Canarsie Pol

STA

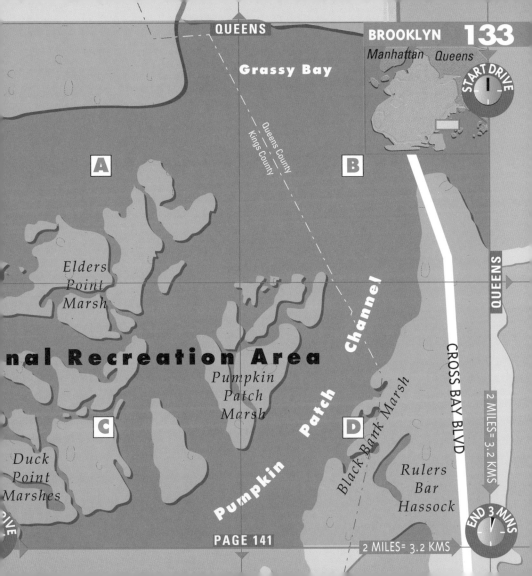

Grassy Bay

Queens County
Kings County

A

B

*Elders
Point
Marsh*

QUEENS

nal Recreation Area

CROSS BAY BLVD

*Pumpkin
Patch
Marsh*

Patch Channel

2 MILES= 3.2 KMS

C

D

Black Bank Marsh

*Duck
Point
Marshes*

*Rulers
Bar
Hassock*

Pumpkin

END 3 MINS

IVE

2 MILES= 3.2 KMS

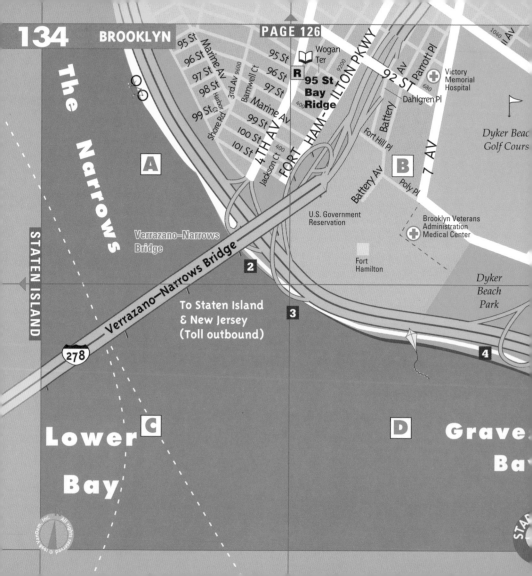

PAGE 126

95 St

96 St

Marine Av

97 St

3rd Av 9600

98 St

Barnwell Ct

99 St

Harbor Ct

Shore Rd

95 St

96 St

97 St

Wogan Ter

R

95 St Bay Ridge

FORT HAMILTON PKWY

92 ST

Parrott Pl

Victory Memorial Hospital

Dahlgren Pl

Battery Av

7 AV

1040 AV

Marine Av

99 St

4TH AV

100 St

101 St

Jackson Ct

Dyker Beach Golf Cours

The Narrows

A

Fort Hill Pl

B

Battery Av

Poly Pl

U.S. Government Reservation

Brooklyn Veterans Administration Medical Center

Verrazano–Narrows Bridge

Fort Hamilton

Dyker Beach Park

STATEN ISLAND

Verrazano–Narrows Bridge

2

To Staten Island & New Jersey (Toll outbound)

3

278

4

Lower

C

Bay

D

Grave

Ba

STAR

83 St
81 St
82 St
84 St
85 St
13 Av
1250
1440
1670
72 St
73 St
74 St
1750
1750

B E N S O N H U R S T

BAY RIDGE PKWY

86 ST
15 Av
16 Av
17 Av
1570
1670
1670
1670
50
B **M** 79 St
76 St
77 St
78 St
79 St
80 St
1760
18 AV

NEW UTRECHT AV

A

8800
213
203
215
Bay 7 St
Bay 8 St
Bay 10 St
Bay 11 St
Bath Av
Bay 13 St
Bay 14 St
Bay 16 St
Bay 17 St
Benson Av
8740
8752
8691
Rutherford Pl
8610
2
B **M** 18 Av
19 Av
20 Av
21 Av
1910
1910
1920
1910

B

1910

2210
2240

CROPSEY AV

Independence
Av

17 Ct

Shore

B A T H

B E A C H

Bay 19 St
Bay 20 St
Bay 22 St
Bay 23 St
Bay 25 St
Bay 26 St
Bay 28 St
Bay 29 St
Benson Av
8630
8710
8900
2
2
2
B **M** 20 Av
2150
2160
2140
2230
2240

BAY PKWY

2230
23 Av
24 Av
2410
B **M**
Bay Pkwy

Benson Av
St
St
8620
8610
Bay 34
Bay 35
Bath Av
Bay 31 St
Bay 32 St
Bay 37 St
Bay 38 St
Bay 40 St
880
8780
25 Av

D

SHORE PKWY (Belt Pkwy)

nd

C

19 La
20 Dr
20 La
21 Dr 21 La
Rd
1460
17 Ct

*Bensonhurst
Park*

Shore Rd
24 Av

5

2 MILES= 3.2 KMS

END 3 MINS

DIVE

2 MILES= 3.2 KMS

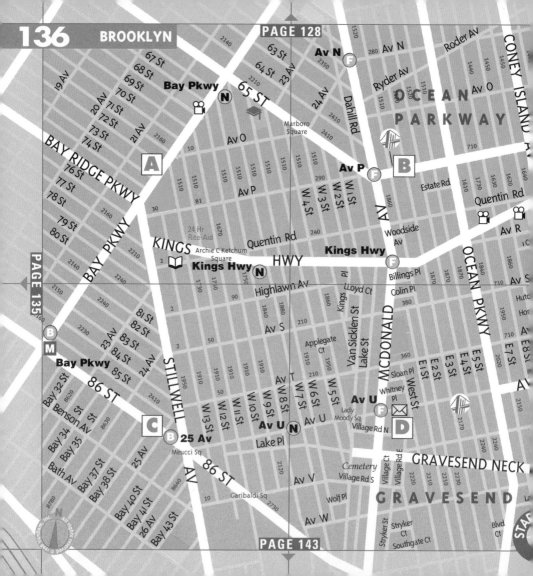

Av N

Av N

Roder Av

CONEY ISLAND AV

Ryder Av

OCEAN

Av O

PARKWAY

67 St
68 St
69 St
70 St
71 St
72 St
73 St
74 St

Bay Pkwy

65 ST

63 St
64 St
23 Av

24 Av

Dahill Rd

Marboro Square

Av O

BAY RIDGE PKWY

76 St
77 St
78 St
79 St
80 St

A

Av P

W 1 St
W 2 St
W 3 St
W 4 St

Av P

B

Estate Rd

Quentin Rd

Av R

Woodside Av

KINGS

24 Hr Rite-Aid

Archie C Ketchum Square

Quentin Rd

240

Kings Hwy

Kings Hwy

HWY

OCEAN PKWY

Kings Hwy

Billings Pl

Av S

Colin Pl

Highlawn Av

LLoyd Ct

Kings Pl

81 St
82 St
83 St
84 St
85 St

23 Av
24 Av

Av S

Applegate Ct

Van Sicklen St
Lake St

MCDONALD

E 5 St
E 4 St
E 3 St
E 2 St
E 1 St

Av S

STILLWELL

Bay Pkwy

B
M

86 ST

W 13 St
W 12 St
W 11 St
W 10 St
W 9 St
W 8 St
W 7 St
W 6 St
W 5 St

Av T

Sloan Pl

West St

C

B 25 Av

Meucci Sq

86 ST

Av U

Av U

Whitney Pl

Av U

Lady Moody Sq

Village Rd N

D

Bay 32 St
Benson Av
Bay 34 St
Bay 35 St
Bay 37 St
Bay 38 St

25 Av

Lake Pl

GRAVESEND NECK

Village Ct
Village Rd E

Bath Av
Bay 40 St
Bay 41 St
26 Av
Bay 43 St

86 ST AV

Garibaldi Sq

Av V

Cemetery
Village Rd S

GRAVESEND

Wolf Pl

Stryker St
Stryker Ct
Southgate Ct

Blvd Ct

Av W

PAGE 130

Quentin Rd
E 31 St
E 32 St
E 33 St
E 34 St
Av R
Marine Pkwy
Madison Pl
Burnett St
Stuart St

Hendrickson St
Coleman St
Kimball St
Ryder St
Fillmore Av
E 38 St
E 37 St
E 36 St
E 35 St

E 52 St
E 53 Pl
E 54 St
E 55 St
E 56 St

E 60 Pl
E 59 Pl
Av R

Kings Plaza
Shopping
Center

MARINE

PARK

Av S

Av T

Strickland
57 Dr
E 57 Pl
Mill Av
National Dr
E 63 St
E 64 St
E 65 St
E 66 St
Whitman Ct
Arkanse

A

Av U

Hendrickson Al

B

*Marine
Park*

MILL

ISLAND

Pratt–White
Field

P

Av V

FLATBUSH AV

GERRITSEN

Av T
Brown St
Batchelder St
Ford St
Coyle St
Haring St

Bragg St

Brigham St

Burnett St

Marine Park
Nature Trail

Marine Park Golf Course

P

Av V

AV

Whitney Av

Marine

Mill Creek

Sheepshead

Bay
Av W

Plumb 2 St
Plumb 1 St

Av X

White

Island

Gerritsen

D

Houses

C

Allen

Aster
Begy
Av
Celeste
Dictum
Ebony Ct
Fane
Garland Ct

Channel Av

Av X

KNAPP ST

Devon Av

Everett Av

GERRITSEN

Creek

Av Y

Fane Ct
Garland Ct
Hazel Ct
Ira Ct
Iowa Ct

Florence Av

Gotham Av

BEACH

Park

PAGE 146

© 1998 Geographia Inc. All rights reserved

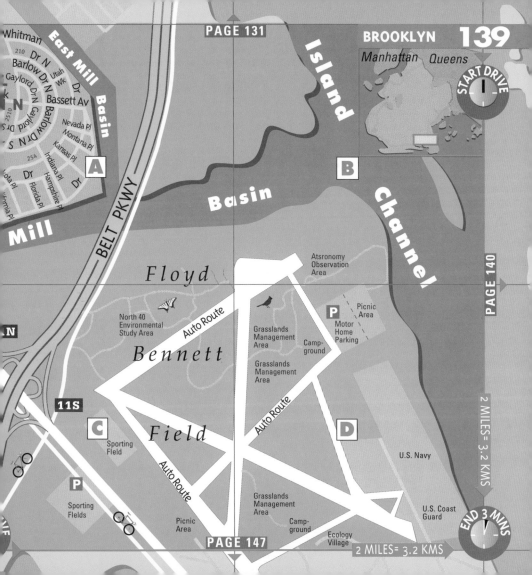

Manhattan Queens

START DRIVE

Whitman
210 Dr N
Barlow Dr N   Utah   Dr
Gaylord Dr N   Wk   Dr
N   Bassett Av
Gaylord Dr N
k
254
Nevada Pl
Montana Pl
Kansas Pl
Indiana Pl
Dr   Florida Pl
Dr   Hampshire Pl
N   Dr S
Mill   East Mill Basin

A

B

Basin

Island

Channel

BELT PKWY

Floyd

Atsronomy
Observation
Area

North 40
Environmental
Study Area

Auto Route

P   Picnic
Area

Motor
Home
Parking

Bennett

Grasslands
Management
Area

Camp-
ground

Grasslands
Management
Area

N

11S

Auto Route

C

Sporting
Fleld

Field

Auto Route

D

U.S. Navy

Auto Route

P

Sporting
Fields

Picnic
Area

Grasslands
Management
Area

Camp-
ground

U.S. Coast
Guard

END 3 MINS

Ecology
Village

2 MILES = 3.2 KMS

2 MILES= 3.2 KMS

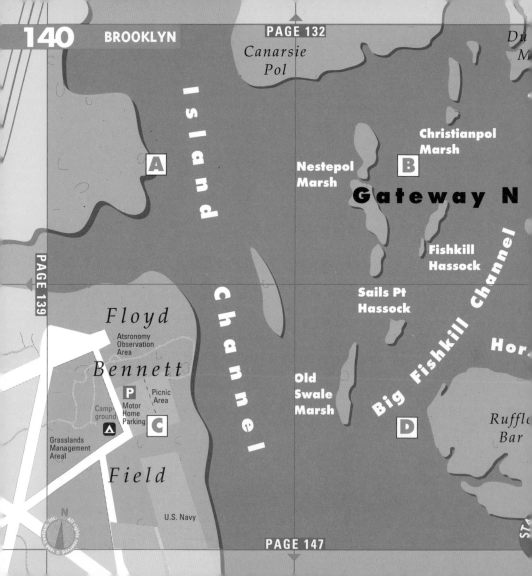

PAGE 132

PAGE 139

Canarsie Pol

Du
M

A

Christianpol Marsh

Nestepol Marsh

B

Gateway N

Fishkill Hassock

I s l a n d

Sails Pt Hassock

C h a n n e l

Floyd

Atsronomy
Observation
Area

Bennett

P

Picnic
Area

Motor
Home
Parking

Camp
ground

C

Grasslands
Management
Areal

Field

Old Swale Marsh

Big Fishkill Channel

Hor.

D

Ruffle Bar

U.S. Navy

N

ST

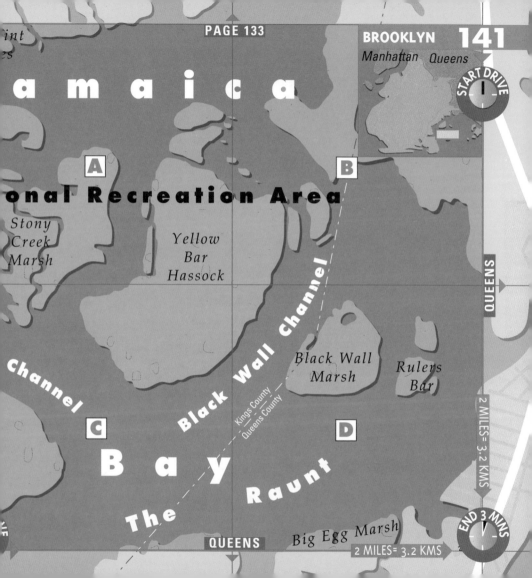

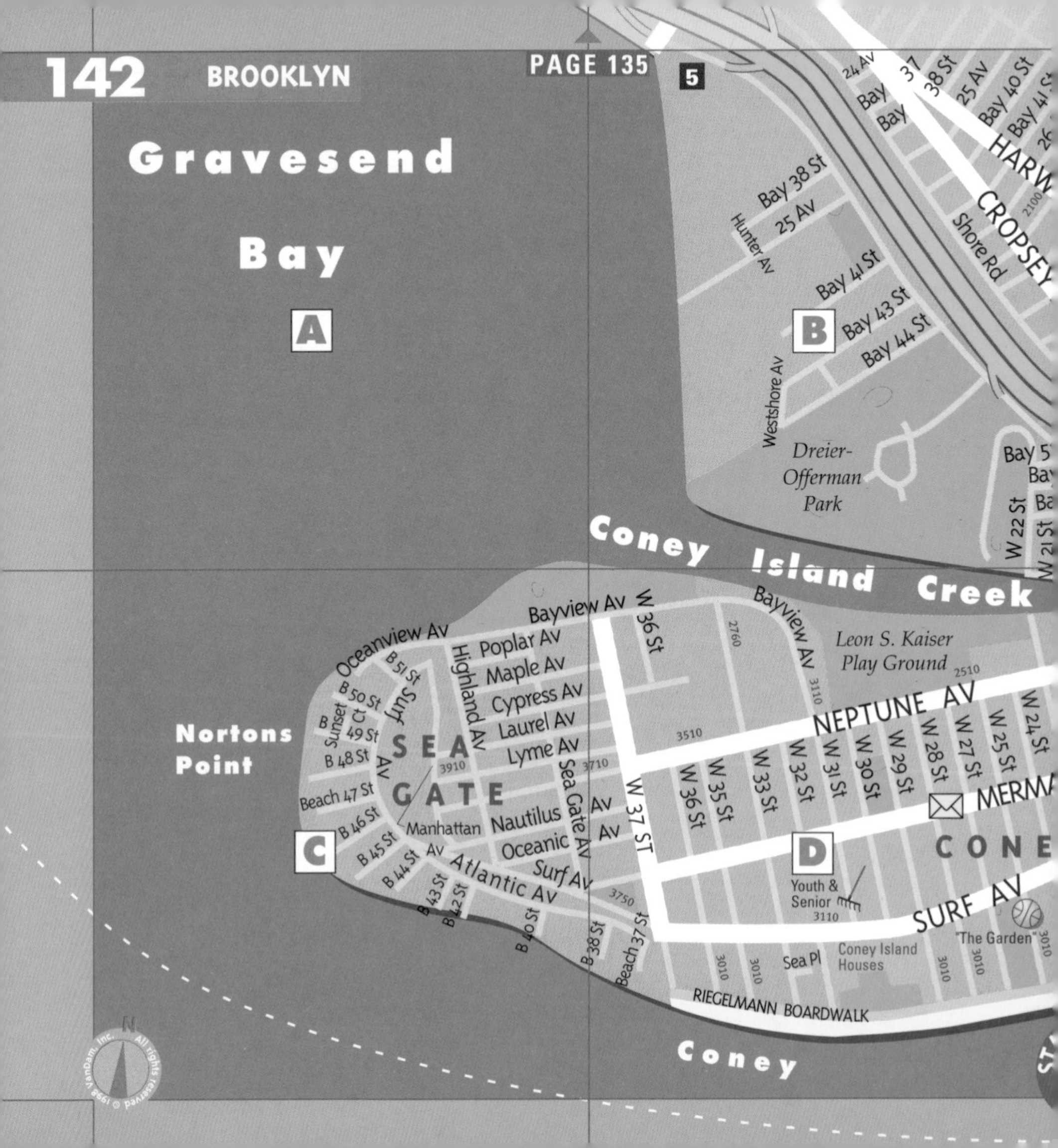

PAGE 135

5

Gravesend

Bay

A

24 Av
37
38 St
Av
Bay
25 Av
Bay 40 St
Bay
Bay 41 St
26

HARW

CROPSEY

Bay 38 St
25 Av

Hunter Av

Shore Rd

B
Bay 41 St
Bay 43 St
Bay 44 St

Westshore Av

Dreier-
Offerman
Park

Bay 5
Bay
W 22 St
W 21 St
Ba

Coney Island Creek

Oceanview Av
Bayview Av
W 36 St
2760
Bayview Av

Leon S. Kaiser
Play Ground
2510

B 51 St
Poplar Av

B 50 Ct
Highland Av
Maple Av
3110

NEPTUNE AV
W 24 St
W 25 St
W 27 St
W 28 St

B 49 St
Sunset
Surf
Cypress Av
3510

W 29 St
W 30 St
W 31 St

**Nortons
Point**
B 48 St
SEA
Laurel Av
W 33 St
W 35 St

Lyme Av
3710

W 32 St
MERMA

GATE
3910
Sea Gate Av

Beach 47 St
W 36 St

B 46 St
Manhattan
Nautilus Av
Oceanic
W 37 ST
D
MERMA

C
B 45 St
Av
Surf Av
3750
Youth &
Senior
3110
C O N E

B 44 St
Atlantic Av
3010
Coney Island
Houses

B 43 St
B 42 St
Beach 49 St
B 38 St
Beach 37
3010
3010
Sea Pl
SURF AV
"The Garden"
3010
3010

RIEGELMANN BOARDWALK

Coney
ST

N

PAGE 137

S H E E P S H E A D

B A Y

Av X

510

Desmond Ct

Ocean Ct

Parkway Ct

Av X

Dunne Ct

Desmond Ct

Dunne Ct

Homecrest

2449

F Av X

Bouck Ct

W 3 St

W 2 St

W 1 St

Manhattan Ct

2410

Brighton Ct

2510

Murdock Ct

Hubbard St

Av Y

Gerald Ct

Kathleen Pl

E 12 St

E 13 St

E 15 St

2543

Sheepshead Bay

Sheepshead

William Ct

Gilmore Ct

Av

2610

D **Q** Bay

OCEAN

E 15 St

E 16 St

E 17 St

E 18 St

E 19 St

E 21 St

E 23

Mansfield

Delamere Pl

Bedford

E 26 St

Av

2650

Av

2660

Jerome Av

Voo

AV

SHELL RD

360

Cobek Ct

Dank Ct

580

AV Z

2510

Murdock Ct

Coney Island Hospital

A

7N Nixon Ct

Manor Ct

Montauk Ct

8

Blake Ct

2770

Shore Pkwy

Lawn Av

E 14 St

B

SHORE PKWY

E 15 St

E 16 St

Rd

EMMONS

Foot Bridge

10 9 8 7 6 5

Atwater Ct

Bokee Ct

Colby Ct

Guider

West Av

2730

7S

Br 3 Rd

370

Br 3 Rd

Banner Av

Br 4 Rd

Br 4 Ter

B 10 Ct

B 10 Path

B 10 Ter

B 10 La

Av

Cass St

B 1 St

B 2 St

B 13 St

B 14 St

SHORE

BLVD

110

Shore

2

500

Blvd

M A N H A T

F **Neptune Av**

Sheepshead Bay

W 5 St

W 3 St

W 2 Pl

W 2 St

N E P T U N E

AV

B 2 Wk

B 2 Wk

B 3 Wk

B 5 Wk

B 7 Wk

Oceanview

B 8 St

B 7 St

B 6 St

Av

B 10 St

Oceanview

B 15 St

Hampton Av

Beaumont

Coleridge

Exeter St

Dover St

Falmouth St

Ocean Av

Girard St

St

B R I G H T O N   B E A C H

Brighton Av

Seabreeze Av

2800

OCEAN

PKWY

Rd

Brighton 1 St

B 1 Pl

B 2 St

B 3 St

B 4 St

B 5 St

BRIGHTON BEACH AV

B 1 Rd

3081

Av

Brighton Beach

Ter

Seacoast

D **Q**

Brighton Beach

Brightwater Av

Gerald H Chambers Sq

Corbin Pl

Amherst

St

St

SHORE WEST END AV

260

ORIENTAL BLVD

260

4220

W 5 St

W 3 St

W 2 St

W 1 St

Ocean Pkwy

Seaside

550

W J Hennesy Square

D

Beach Wk

Brightwater Ct

BOARDWALK EAST

Seabreeze Wk

SURF

AV

ESPLANADE

M

B

New York Aquarium

Park

C

Brighton Beach

D

BOARDWALK

ST

PAGE 143

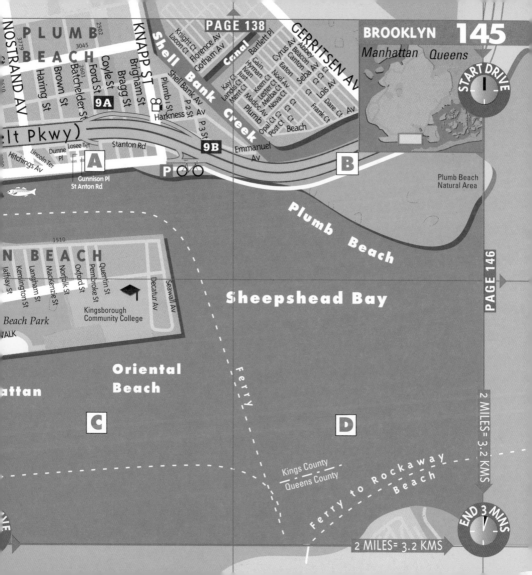

PLUMB
BEACH

NOSTRAND

KNAPP ST

Shell Bank

2502
3045
3170

Knight Ct
Lacon Ct
Florence AV
Cotham Av

Bartlett Pl

GERRITSEN AV

Canal

Coyle St
Ford St
Batchelder St
Brown St
Haring St

Bragg St
Brigham St

Plumb 1 St
Shell Bank Av
P 2 St
Harkness Av
P 3 St

Gain
Hyman
Ivan
Merit Ct

Cyrus Av
Abbey
Beacon
Canton
Eaton
Seba

Kay Ct
Landis Ct

Noel Av
Lester Ct
Keen Ct
Madoc Av
Melba Ct
Nova Ct
Opal Ct
Post Ct

Ct

Av
Gt
Ct

Lois Av
Dare Ct
Frank Ct

9A

9B

Plumb

Beach

(lt Pkwy)

Hitchings Av
Lincoln Pl
Dunne Pl
Losee Ter

Stanton Rd

Gunnison Pl
St Anton Rd

A

P

Emmanuel
Av

B

BROOKLYN

Manhattan Queens

START DRIVE

Plumb Beach
Natural Area

PAGE 146

Plumb   Beach

1510

N BEACH

Jaffray St
Kensington St
Langham St
MacKenzie St

Norfolk St
Oxford St
Pembroke St
Quentin St

Decatur Av

Seawall Av

Kingsborough
Community College

Sheepshead Bay

Beach Park

WALK

**Oriental
Beach**

attan

C

2 MILES= 3.2 KMS

D

Ferry

Kings County
Queens County

Ferry to Rockaway   Beach

END 3 MINS

2 MILES= 3.2 KMS

BROOKLYN

PAGE 138

Brigham St

Plumb St

Shell Bank Av

Shell Bank Creek

P 2 St

Harkness Av

P 3 St

9B

Emmanuel Av

Kay Ct
Ivan Ct
Landis Ct
Fisk Ct
Merit Ct

Cytus Av
Keen Ct
Lester Ct
Madoc Av
Nova Ct
Opal Ct
Post Ct

Beacon Ct
Noel Av
Melba Ct

Abbey Av
Canton Ct
Sedra Ct
Frank Ct

Lois Av
Dare Ct

Eaton Ct

Plumb Beach

P

Plumb Beach Channel

BELT PKWY

P

A

Plumb Beach

Dead Horse Bay

Barren Island Marina

B

Plumb Beach Natural Area

Dead Horse Inlet

PAGE 145

Decatur Av

Seawall Av

Kingsborough Community College

Oriental Beach

Ferry

C

Kings County
Queens County

D

Ferry to

R o

QUEENS

STA

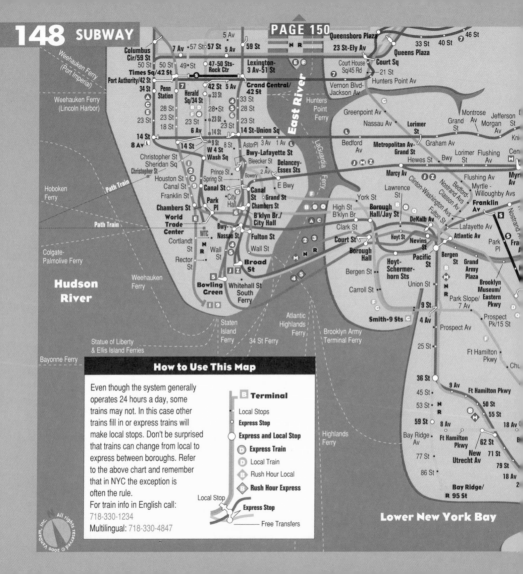

East River

Hudson River

Lower New York Bay

Weehauken Ferry (Port Imperial)

Weehauken Ferry (Lincoln Harbor)

Hoboken Ferry

Path Train

Path Train

Colgate-Palmolive Ferry

Bayonne Ferry

Weehauken Ferry

Staten Island Ferry

34 St Ferry

Statue of Liberty & Ellis Island Ferries

Atlantic Highlands Ferry

Brooklyn Army Terminal Ferry

Highlands Ferry

Stations

7 Av · 57 St · 5 Av · 5 Av
Columbus Cir/59 St
50 St · 50 St · 49 St · 47-50 Sts-Rock Ctr
Times Sq/42 St
Port Authority/42 St
34 St · Penn Station · 7 · 42 St · 5 Av · Grand Central/42 St
Herald Sq/34 St · 33 St · 33 St
28 St · 28 St · 28 St
23 St · 23 St · 23 St · 23 St
18 St
14 St · 6 Av · 14 St · 14 St-Union Sq
8 Av · 14 St · 8 St · Astor Pl · 3 Av · 1 Av
W 4 St · Wash Sq
Christopher St Sheridan Sq
Christopher St
Houston St · Prince St · Bwy-Lafayette St
Bleecker St · Delancey-Essex Sts
Canal St · Spring St · Bowery · 2 Av
Franklin St
Canal St · Canal St · Grand St
Chambers St · City Hall · Chambers St
Park Pl
World Trade Center · WTC · B'klyn Br./City Hall
Cortlandt St · Bwy-Nassau St · Fulton St
Rector St · Wall St · Wall St
Broad St
Bowling Green · Whitehall St South Ferry

59 St · 59 St
23 St-Ely Av · Queensboro Plaza · 33 St · 40 St · 46 St
Queens Plaza
Court House Sq/45 Rd · Court Sq
21 St
Vernon Blvd-Jackson Av · Hunters Point Av
Greenpoint Av
Nassau Av · Montrose Av · Jefferson St · Morgan Av
Bedford Av · Lorimer St · Grand St
Metropolitan Av-Grand St · Graham Av
Hewes St · Bwy · Lorimer St · Flushing Av
Marcy Av · Flushing Av · Myrtle-Willoughby Avs · Myrtle Av
York St · Bedford-Nostrand Avs · Franklin Av
Lawrence St · Clinton-Washington Avs · Nostrand Av
High St B'klyn Br · Borough Hall/Jay St · Fulton St · Lafayette Av
Clark St · DeKalb Av · Atlantic Av
Court St · Hoyt St · Nevins St · Park Pl · Franklin Av
Borough Hall · Pacific St
Bergen St · Hoyt-Schermerhorn Sts · Bergen St · Grand Army Plaza
Carroll St · Union St · Brooklyn Museum/Eastern Pkwy
9 St · Park Slope/7 Av · Prospect Pk/15 St
Smith-9 Sts · 4 Av · Prospect Av
25 St
36 St · 9 Av · Ft Hamilton Pkwy
45 St · 50 St
53 St · 55 St
59 St · 8 Av · 18 Av
Bay Ridge Av · Ft Hamilton Pkwy · 62 St · 71 St · 79 St
77 St · New Utrecht Av · 18 Av
86 St
Bay Ridge/R 95 St

How to Use This Map

Even though the system generally operates 24 hours a day, some trains may not. In this case other trains fill in or express trains will make local stops. Don't be surprised that trains can change from local to express between boroughs. Refer to the above chart and remember that in NYC the exception is often the rule.

For train info in English call:
718-330-1234
Multilingual: 718-330-4847

Terminal
· Local Stops
· **Express Stop**
Express and Local Stop
○ **Express Train**
○ **Local Train**
○ **Rush Hour Local**
◇ **Rush Hour Express**

Local Stop

Express Stop

Free Transfers

QUEENS

MANHATTAN

BROOKLYN

Middle Village/
Metropolitan Av

111 St

104 St

Ozone Park/
Lefferts Blvd

Fresh Pond Rd

Woodhaven Blvd

111 St
(Greenwood Av)

Forest Av

85 St-Forest Pkwy

Seneca Av

75 St

104 St (Oxford Av)

Cypress Hills

Rockaway
Blvd

open 11am-7pm
racing days

Shuttle Bus-
Q3, Q10, B15

Wyckoff Av

Crescent St

88 St

Aqueduct
Racetrack

Halsey St

Wilson Av

Norwood Av

80 St

JFK
Airport

Bushwick Av-Aberdeen St

Cleveland St

Grant Av

Aqueduct/
N. Conduit
Av

ates Halsey
v   St

Euclid
Av

cko   Chauncey St

Van Siclen Av

Alabama Av

Shepherd Av

Howard Beach
JFK Airport

Bwy-
Eastern Pkwy

Rock-
away
Av

Ralph Av

Bwy-
East New
York

Atlantic Av

Liberty
Av

Van Siclen Av

Church Av

Sutter Av

Rockaway
Av

Van Siclen
Av

New Lots Av

Crown Hts/
Utica Av

Pennsylvania Av

ngston
Av

Sutter Av
Rutland Rd

Saratoga
Av

Junius
St

Livonia Av

New Lots Av

strand
Av

President St

E 105 St

Sterling St

Winthrop St

Church Av

Canarsie/
Rockaway Pkwy

Beverly Rd

Newkirk Av

Jamaica
Bay

side Av

hurch Av

Beverly Rd

Cortelyou Rd

Newkirk Av

Brooklyn
College/
Flatbush Av

Av H

Av J

Av M

BROOKLYN

ay Pkwy

Kings Hwy

Av N

Broad Channel

Far Rockaway/
Mott Av

Av P

Kings Hwy

Av U

Beach 25 St

Neck Rd

Beach 36 St

wy

Av U

Sheepshead
Bay

Av X

Beach 90 St

Beach 44 St

Av U

25 Av

86 St

Neptune
Av

Brighton Beach

Beach 98 St

Beach
67 St

Beach 60 St

Bay 50 St

Ocean Pkwy

Beach 105 St

oney Island/
Stillwell Av

NY Aquarium/W 8 St

Rockaway Park
Beach 116 St

Atlantic Ocean

THE BRONX

MANHATTAN
Central Park

Hudson River

East River

La Guardia Airport

Randall's Island

Roosevelt Island

Astoria/
Ditmars Blvd

Wakefield/241 St
Eastchester/Dyre Av
Nereid Av
233 St
225 St
219 St
Gun Hill Rd
Burke Av
Allerton Av
Pelham Pkwy
Bronx Park East
E. 180 St
W. Farms Sq-
E. Tremont Av
174 St
Freeman St
Simpson St
Intervale Av
Prospect Av
Jackson Av

Baychester Av
Pelham Bay Pk
Gun Hill Rd
Pelham Pkwy
Morris Pk
Buhre Av
Middletown Rd
Westchester Sq-
E. Tremont Av
Zerega Av
Castle Hill Av
Parkchester/
E.177 St
St. Lawrence Av
Morrison-Sound View Avs
Elder Av
Whitlock Av
Hunts Point Av
Longwood Av
E. 149 St
St. Mary's St-E. 143 St

Woodlawn
Mosholu Pkwy
Lehman College/
Bedford Pk Blvd
Kingsbridge Rd
Fordham Rd
183 St
Burnside Av
176 St
Mt Eden Av
170 St
167 St
Yankee Stad./
161 St
155 St
145 St
135 St
125 St

205 St
Norwood
Bedford Park Blvd
Kingsbridge Rd
Fordham Rd
182-183 St
Tremont Av
174-175 St
170 St
167 St

Van Cortlandt Pk/
242 St
238 St
231 St
Marble Hill/225 St
215 St
207 St
Dyckman St
191 St
181 St

207 St
Dyckman St
190 St
181 St
175 St
Washington Hts/
168 St
Amsterdam Av-163 St
157 St
145 St
City Coll./
137 St
125 St
Columbia Univ./
116 St
103 St
96 St
86 St
79 St
72 St

Harlem/
148 St
145 St
135 St
125 St
116 St
110 St
(Central Park North)
103 St
96 St
86 St
Mus. of Nat. History/81 St
72 St
Lincoln Ctr/
66 St
Columbus Cir/59 St
50 St
Times Sq/42 St
Port Authority/42 St
34 St
Penn Station
28 St
23 St

Grand Concourse-
149 St
3 Av-
149 St
Grand Concourse-
138 St
3 Av-138 St
Brook Av
Cypress Av

116 St
110 St
103 St
96 St
77 St
Hunter Coll./
68 St
59 St
Lexington Av
Lexington Av
5 Av
57 St
5 Av
47-50 Sts-
Rock Ctr
Lexington-
3 Av-51 St
Grand Central/
42 St
42 St
5 Av
7 Av
57 St

Herald Sq/34 St
33 St
28 St
23 St
33 St
28 St
23 St
23 St

LaGuardia Ferry

Weehauken Ferry
(Port Imperial)
Weehauken Ferry
(Lincoln Harbor)

Astoria Blvd
30 Av
Steinway St
Broadway
36 Av
39 Av
36 St
21 St
Queensbridge
Queensboro Plaza
23 St-Ely Av
Court House
Sq/45 Rd
Court Sq
21 St
Vernon Blvd-
Jackson Av
Hunters Point Av
Greenpoint Av
Nassau Av
Hunters Point Ferry

Northern Blvd
46 St
65 St
74 St
Bway
Woodside
52 St
61 St
46 St
40 St
33 St
Queens Plaza
Q33

THE
BRONX

QUEENS

MANHATTAN

Express Trains	Local Trains	Rush Hour Trains
Here's how New Yorkers refer to the lines of their system		
❷ ❸ ❹ ❺	❶ ❾ ❻ ❼	⬥ **S** Brooklyn & The Bronx
Ⓐ Ⓔ Queens	Ⓐ Brooklyn after 9 pm & weekends Ⓖ Ⓔ Manhattan Ⓢ	⬥ **A** Rockaway
Ⓑ Manhattan & Bklyn eves	Ⓑ Brooklyn 36 St - Coney Island late nights Ⓒ	⬥ Manhattan 59 St - Bklyn 36 St
Ⓓ Manhattan	Ⓓ Brooklyn & The Bronx Ⓕ	⬥ Manhattan 59 St - 168 St
		⬥ Manh & Bronx Ⓒ Bklyn
Ⓙ Ⓩ Queens Myrtle-Marcy Av, Manhattan	Ⓙ evenings Ⓜ	⬥ Queens 71 Av - Queens Plaza
Ⓚ No service after 9pm. Queens use B train, Brooklyn use D train.	Ⓝ Ⓡ Ⓢ Shuttle	⬥ **N** Brooklyn ⬥ **N** Queens & Manhattan
	Ⓛ	

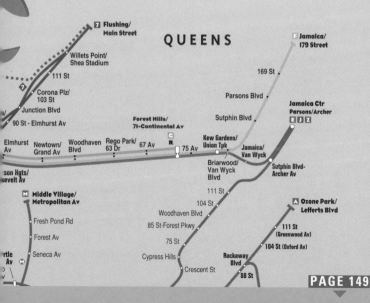

QUEENS

7 Flushing/ Main Street

Willets Point/ Shea Stadium

111 St

Corona Plz/ 103 St

Junction Blvd

90 St - Elmhurst Av

Elmhurst Av

Newtown/ Grand Av

Woodhaven Blvd

Rego Park/ 63 Dr

67 Av

75 Av

Forest Hills/ 71-Continental Av

Kew Gardens/ Union Tpk

Jamaica/ Van Wyck

Briarwood/ Van Wyck Blvd

169 St

Parsons Blvd

Sutphin Blvd

Jamaica/ 179 Street

Jamaica Ctr Parsons/Archer
E J Z

Sutphin Blvd-Archer Av

...son Hgts/ ...sevelt Av

M Middle Village/ Metropolitan Av

Fresh Pond Rd

Forest Av

Seneca Av

...rtle Av

111 St

104 St

Woodhaven Blvd

85 St-Forest Pkwy

75 St

Cypress Hills

Crescent St

Rockaway Blvd

88 St

A Ozone Park/ Lefferts Blvd

111 St (Greenwood Av)

104 St (Oxford Av)

PAGE 149

ABBREVIATIONS

Al	Alley	Pl	Place
Av	Avenue	Plz	Plaza
Bd, Blvd	Point	Pt	Point
	Boulevard	Rd	Road
Br	Bridge	Sq	Square
Cir	Circle	St	Street
Cres	Crescent	Ter	Terrace
Ct	Court	Tri	Triangle
Dr	Drive	Tun	Tunnel
Expwy		Wk	Walk
	Expressway	Wy	Way
Ft	Fort		
Hts	Heights	MA	Manhattan
Hwy	Highway	NJ	New Jersey
La	Lane	QS	Queens
Pkwy	Parkway	SI	Staten Island

FINDING A STREET

Simply turn to page and locate the street or avenue in grids **A,B,C** or **D**.

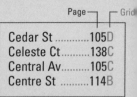

Page ─┐   ┌─ Grid

Cedar St	105D
Celeste Ct	138C
Central Av	105C
Centre St	114B

BAM
Brooklyn Academy of Music

America's premier contemporary performing arts and cultural center

film

opera

theater

dance

music

BAM Rose Cinemas

Brooklyn's premier movie house dedicated to independent first-run films, classics, documentaries, retrospectives and festivals.
Advance Tickets 718.623.2770
BAMcinématek repertory programming 718.623.4157

BAMcafé

Dinner and drinks Tue—Sat 5—11 pm Sunday brunch 12—4pm
Live music and spoken word Thu—Sat nights. No cover!
Info 718.636 4139

Shakespeare & Co. BAMshop

A new place to find a great selection of books, CDs, and BAMgifts. Located in BAMcafé.

30 Lafayette Avenue, Brooklyn, NY 718.636.4100 / www.bam.org

Hudson River

MANHATTAN

JOE DIMAGGIO HWY

8 AV
7 AV
6 AV
BWY
3 AV
1 AV
E 14 ST

BROADWAY
BOWERY
HOUSTON

FDR DR

East River

Pulaski Bridge

GREEN-POINT

N 9 ST

NORTH SIDE

BROO

32 GR

Williamsburg Bridge

SOUTH SIDE

WILLIAMS

Brooklyn Bridge
Manhattan Bridge

DUMBO VINEGAR HILL

NAVY YARD

31

FLUSHIN

Brooklyn Battery Tunnel (toll)

FULTON FERRY

28

BROOKLYN HEIGHTS

BQE

278

MYRTL

DOWNTOWN

29

FORT GREENE

CLINTO HILL

COLUMBIA

27

278

ATLANTIC AV

FLATBUSH AV

WASHINGTON AV

BEDFORD AV

Governors Island

26

COBBLE HILL

BOERUM HILL

PROSPECT HEIGHTS

CARROLL GARDENS

GOWANUS

RED HOOK

Upper New York Bay

PARK SLOPE

Prospect Park

PROSPECT HEIGHTS

1

23

2A

3 AV

5 AV

9 ST

WINDSOR TERRACE

EMPIRE

GOWANUS EXPWY

278

2B

27

PROSPECT EXPWY

PROSPE LEFFER GARDE

GOWANUS EXPWY

Greenwood
Cemetery

1

PROSPECT
PARK SOUT

CHURCH AV

OCEAN AV

SUNSET
PARK

5 AV

7 AV

KENSINGTON

DITMAS
PARK

BAY RIDGE

I-278

FORT HAMILTON PKWY

NEW UTRECHT AV

McDONALD AV

BOROUGH
PARK

OCEAN AV

BAY
RIDGE

PKWY

65 ST

18 AV

CONEY ISLAND AV

BELT PKWY

86 ST

4 AV

MAPLETON

MIDW

DYKER
HEIGHTS

92 ST

BENSONHURST

OCEAN
PARKWAY

OCEAN PKWY

FORT
HAMILTON

Dyker
Beach
G.C

86 ST

NEW
UTRECHT

BAY PKWY

AV P

M

KINGS HWY

3

CROPSEY AV

BELT PKWY

2

STILLWELL AV

HOMECREST

I-278

4

BATH
BEACH

GRAVESEND NEC

AV U

Verrazano
Narrows
Bridge (toll)

5

HARWAY AV

GRAVESEND

SHELL RD

SH

Gravesend
Bay

Dreier-
Offerman
Pk

6

OCEAN PKWY

AV

7 **8**

SEA
GATE

NEPTUNE AV

W. 37

Seaside
Pk

BRIGHTON
BEACH AV

SURF AV

CONEY ISLAND

BRIGH
BEAC

GREAT MINDS
DON'T
THINK ALIKE

At Bell Atlantic we believe in the power of diversity and the power of the individual. It is individual thinking from a diverse group of people working together that provides fresh new ideas and gives us a competitive edge. At Bell Atlantic you're in good company.

Bell Atlantic

Get away from it all...

Christine M. Douglas

Loose yourself in the beauty of the Brooklyn Botanic Garden.

And while you're here, check out our Garden Gift Shop for
great gardening supplies and gifts, plus a super selection of books and toys.

BROOKLYN BOTANIC GARDEN

900 WASHINGTON AVENUE, BROOKLYN, NEW YORK 11225, 718-623-7200

To reach the Garden by subway take the (2) or (3) to Eastern Parkway/Brooklyn Museum
Station or the (D) or (Q) to Prospect Park Station. By bus, use the B41, B47, B48 or B71.

Explore bbg online at www.bbg.org.

CONNECT @ CITY TECH

NEW YORK CITY
TECHNICAL COLLEGE
300 JAY STREET • BROOKLYN, N.Y. 11201

718.260.5500
www.nyctc.cuny.edu

FIND A STREET

Simply turn to the page and locate your street, road, or place in grids A,B,C or D.

Long thoroughfares are indexed with a range of page and grid coordinates that indicate the start and end of the road.

Rockaway Pkwy .....
.....117D-132A

For a quick overview of the highway system refer to page 100.

TOMMY, FUBU, VICTORIA, CALVIN, RALPH, LEVI AND _____.

(your name here)

With over 140 great stores, including Macy's, Sears, Old Navy, Gap, Ann Taylor Loft and Modell's, shopping in Brooklyn has never been better. So, for the brands you want at the prices you love, visit Kings Plaza today. You'll be in good company.

KINGS PLAZA

Macy's, Sears & 140 Specialty Stores. Flatbush Ave. and Ave. U 718-253-6842

Visitor Services

All phone numbers are within area code (718) unless otherwise noted.

EMERGENCIES

AAA Road Service
800-222-4357

Ambulance, Fire, Police
911

Animal Affairs-Veterinary Public Health
212-676-2120

Animal Bites
212-676-2483

Arson Hotline
722-3600

Battered Women
800-621-4673

Coast Guard
800-735-3415

Child Abuse
800-342-3720

Domestic Violence
800-621-4673

Drug Abuse
800-395-3400

Emergency Children's Services
212-966-8000

Emergency Medical Technician Info
416-7000

Hazardous Materials Complaints (24/7)
337-4357

Locksmith (24/7)
898-3333

Park Emergencies (24/7) 800-201-7275

Pharmacies (24/7)
Bay Ridge:
748-8184
Bensonhurst:
331-2019
Flatbush:
951-6869

Poison Control Center (24/7)
212-764-7667

Rape Hotline
212-577-7777

Sex Crimes Reports Line
212-267-7273

Suicide Prevention
212-532-2400

Victim Services Hotline
212-577-7777

ESSENTIALS

AAA
212-757-2000

ChequePoint USA
212-869-6281

Convention & Visitor's Bureau
212-484-1222

Customs (24hr)
800-697-3662

Directory Info
411

Foreign Exchange Rates
212-883-0400

Hotel Reservations (Brooklyn Marriott)
888-436-3759

Immigration
212-264-5650

Jacob Javits Convention Center
212-216-2000

Lost Travelers Checks
• AMEX
800-221-7282
• Citicorp
800-645-6556
• VISA
800-227-6811

Movies
777-FILM

NYC On Stage
212-768-1818

Passport Info
834-3052

Post Office (Main—Manhattan)
212-967-8585

Telegrams (Western Union)
800-325-6000

Time
976-1616

UN Information
212-963-1234

Weather
976-1212

TOURS & EXCURSIONS

All American Stage Tours
800-735-8530

Art Tours
212-239-4160

Big Apple Greeter
212-669-2896

Big Onion Tours
212-439-1090

Brooklyn Attitude
398-0939

Brooklyn Borough Hall
875-4047

Brooklyn Brewery
486-7422

Brooklyn Center for the Urban Environment
788-8500

Brooklyn Historical Society
254-9830

Brooklyn Information & Culture (BRIC)
855-7882 ext. 51

Circle Line
212-563-3200

Doorways to Design
339-1542

Ellis Island & Statue of Liberty Ferry
212-269-5755

Gray Line NY Tours
212-397-2600

Hoboken Ferry (NJ)
201-420-4422

Liberty Helicopters
212-967-6464

NY Apple Tours
800-876-9868

NY Waterway
800-53-FERRY

Seaport Music Cruises
212-630-8888

Seastreak
800-262-8743

Spirit Cruises
212-727-2789

Tours of Hasidic Crown Heights
953-5244 or
800-838-TOUR

Urban Explorations
721-5254

Wild Foods & Ecology Tours
291-6825

World Yacht Cruises
212-630-8100

TRANSPORTION

Airlines–Domestic
• American
800-433-7300
• Continental
800-523-3273

• Delta
800-221-1212
• Northwest
800-441-1818
• TWA
800-221-2000
• United
800-241-6522
• USAir
800-428-4322

Airlines–Foreign
• Aeromexico
800-237-6639
• Air Canada
800-776-3000
• Air France
800-321-4538
• ANA-ALL Nippon
800-235-9262
• British Airways
800-247-9297
• Lufthansa
800-645-3880

Bus & Subway
• Main 330-1234
• Access - Disabled
596-8585
• George Washington Bridge Bus Station
212-564-1114
• Greyhound
800-231-2222

Then.

ConEd Billing

ConEd Repairs

ConEd Installation

ConEd Bronx

ConEd Steam

ConEd Gas

ConEd Maintenance

ConEd Westchester

ConEd Electric

ConEd Brooklyn

ConEd Staten Island

ConEd Safety

ConEd Distribution

ConEd Manhattan

ConEd Queens

Now.

ConEd Direct

Introducing ConEd Direct. In a world gone mad with phone numbers, Con Edison announces just one convenient, toll-free number. One number to reach all of Con Edison's customer service departments, 1-800-75-CONED. It's easy to remember, too. Call 1-800-75-CONED for your customer service needs 24 hours a day, 7 days a week.

Con Edison

The Company You Know.
The People You Trust.

1-800-75-CONED

Now One Call Solves It All.

www.coned.com

The **Brooklyn** *Historical Society*

Discovers the Past

embracing the people, places and events of importance in Brooklyn's history

Celebrates the Present

presenting innovative educational programming and exhibits that examine Brooklyn's rich heritage

Shapes the Future

connecting the library and museum collections with state-of-the-art technology, cutting-edge interactive exhibits and rewarding educational programming

The Brooklyn Historical Society
2 MetroTech Center, Suite 4200   Brooklyn, NY 11201
Telephone 718.254.9830   Facsimile 718.254.9869

- Hampton Jitney
  800-936-0440
- Port Authority
  Bus Terminal
  212-564-8484

Ferries

- Ellis Island
  212-269-5755
- Harbor Shuttle
  888-254-RIDE
- NY Waterways
  800-53-FERRY
- Seastreak
  800-262-8743
- Staten Island
  815-BOAT
- Statue of
  Liberty
  212-269-5755

Helicopter

- Helicopter
  Flight
  Services
  212-355-0801
- Liberty
  212-487-4777

JFK Airport

- Main
  244-4444
- Train to Plane
  858-7272

**LaGuardia
Airport**

- Main
  476-5000
- Airport Bus
  533-3705
- Ferry
  800-53-FERRY

- Parking
  533-3850

Newark Airport

- Main
  973-961-6000
- Airport Bus
  973-242-0394
- Parking
  973-961-4750

**NY Passenger
Ship Terminal**
212-246-5451

**Roosevelt Island
Tram**
212-832-4543

Trains

- Amtrak
  800-523-8720
  212-582-6875
- LIRR
  217-5477
- Metro North
  800-638-7646
- NJ Transit
  800-626-7433
- PATH
  800-234-7284

**BUSINESS &
CONSUMER**

**Better Business
Bureau**
212-533-6200

**Brooklyn Chamber
of Commerce**
875-1000

**Brooklyn Economic
Development
Corporation (BEDC)**
522-4600

**Brooklyn Goes
Global**
875-1000

**Caribbean
American
Chamber of
Commerce
& Industry (CACCI)**
834-4544

Consumer Affairs
212-487-4444

**Gas, Electric,
Water Complaints**
800-342-3377

**Small Business
Administration
(SBA)** 212-264-4354

**South Brooklyn
Local
Development Corp.
(SBLDC)**
852-0328

Taxi Complaints
212-221-8294

GOVERNMENT

Borough President
802-3700

City Council
212-788-7100

Mayor's Office
212-788-7585

**HEALTH &
HUMAN
SERVICES**

AIDS Hotline
800-462-6787

**Alcoholics
Anonymous**
212-647-1680

Bail
212-669-2879

**Domestic
Violence Hotline**
800-621-4673

**Department for
the Aging**
212-442-1000

Disabled Info
212-229-3000

**Gay and Lesbian
Health Concerns**
212-788-4310

**Health Department
Complaints**
212-442-9666

Health Info (24/7)
212-434-2000

Legal Aid Society
212-577-3300

Medicaid
291-1900

Medicare
800-638-6833

Senior Citizens
212-442-1000

Salvation Army
212-337-7200

Social Security
291-1900

LIBRARIES

**Brooklyn
Business Library**
623-7000

**Brooklyn
Public Library**
230-2100

**PARKING &
TRAFFIC**

Potholes
225-5368

Sidewalks
225-5368

Towed-Away
212-971-0700

Registration Plates
966-6155

Parking Violations
422-7800

TAXES

- City Tax (24hr)
  935-6736
- Federal (IRS)
  800-829-1040
- State Tax
  800-225-5829

UTILITIES

Brooklyn Union
643-4050

Con Edison
800-75-CON-ED
800-752-6633

Bell Atlantic
890-1550

**WEBSITES
BROOKLYN**

**Brooklyn Botanic
Garden**
www.bbg.org

Brooklyn Chamber
www.brooklyn
chamber.com

**BrooklynChildren's
Museum**
www.bchildmus.org

**Brooklyn
Information
& Culture (BRIC)**
www.brooklynx.org
/tourism

**The Brooklyn
Museum of Art**
brooklynart.org

**Brooklyn Public
Library**
brooklynpublic
library.org

Coney Island
coneyisland.
brooklyn.ny.us

**Courier-Life
Newspapers**
brooklynny.com

Prospect Park
prospectpark.org

Prospect Park Zoo
wcs.org

1010 President St
brooklyn.net

NOTES:

ATTRACTIONS

ARTS & SCIENCES

Art Galleries

Belanthi Gallery
142 Court St
@ Pacific St
624-9420
• A neighborhood fixture of more than 20 years featuring contemporary art in all media, poetry readings, music lessons and recitals. **107C**

Brooklyn Brewery
118 N 11 St
(bet. Berry & Wythe Sts) 486-7422
• This neighborhood institution is a throw-back to a time when Brooklyn housed more than 200 breweries. Offers free samples of specialty beers and weekend facility tours. **102D**

The Center for Art & Culture of Bedford Stuyvesant
1368 Fulton St
(bet. New York & Brooklyn Av)
636-6949
• African and African–American art gallery in a historic neighborhood. **116B**

Ifetayo Cultural Arts Facility
929 Flatbush Av
(bet. Church & Snyder Avs)
800-220-7430 **122B**

Lewis Gallery
525 Atlantic Av
(bet. Third & Fourth Avs) 624-8372
• An underground museum shop and source of African-American art. They also do custom framing. **107D**

The Rotunda Gallery
33 Clinton St
(bet. Pierrepont St & Cadman Plz W)
875-4047
• Works by Brooklyn artists and arts education for children. **108B**

Simmons Collection
1063 Fulton St
@ Classon Av
230-0933
• African art museum and gift shop. **110D**

Skylight Gallery
1368 Fulton St–3 flr (Restoration Plz off New York Av)
636-6976
• Features the work of emerging local artists in a variety of media. **116B**

NY Glass Center
647 Fulton St @
Rockwell Pl
625-3685 **110C**

Cultural Organizations

The Brooklyn Arts Council
195 Cadman Plz W
(Brooklyn War Memorial Building)
625-0080
• Cultural resource center with its own calendar of Brooklyn art activities. **108B**

Brooklyn Information & Culture (BRIC)
855-7882, ext. 51
• Your best bet for tourist info! Call for "Meet Me in Brooklyn," a free, quarterly calendar of cultural events.

Brooklyn Waterfront Artists Coalition
596-2507
• Presents several shows featuring works by Brooklyn artists. **107A**

Williamsburg Art & Historical Center
135 Broadway
@ Bedford Av
486-7372
• Produces eclectic art shows and performances. **104A**

Museums

The Brooklyn Children's Museum
145 Brooklyn Av
@ St. Mark's Av
735-4423
• Opened in 1899, this is the world's first museum created specifically for children. Features interactive exhibitions and programs to aid children in their exploration of science. **116B**

Brooklyn Museum of Art (BMA)
200 Eastern Pkwy
638-5000
• Opened in 1897, BMA is one of the world's great museums. It has a multi–discipline collection of more than 1.5 million items including its vast holdings of Egyptian artifacts. **116A**

The Brooklyn Historical Society
128 Pierrepont St
624-0890
• Features a range of exhibits of Brooklyn's history, as well as a research library with the largest Brooklyn collection in existence. **108D**

Harbor Defense Museum
101 St & Fort Hamilton Pkwy
630-4349
• Within the walls of a former flank defense battery the military museum exhibits military weaponry. **134A**

The New York Transit Museum
Boerum Pl
@ Schermerhorn St
243-8601, 694-5102
• This 1930s subway station turned museum showcases vintage railway cars and exhibitions tracing the transit system's history. **108B**

Performing Arts

Arts at St. Ann's
157 Montague St
834-8794
• This Gothic Revival style church is host to a calendar of classical music, jazz, blues, opera, dance and theater. **108B**

Bargemusic Ltd.
Fulton Ferry Landing
624-4061
• A year-round program of chamber music in a floating concert hall, a former Erie-Lackawanna coffee barge. **107A**

Billie Holiday Theatre
1368 Fulton St
@ New York Av
57-6363
• Award–winning theatre with great reputation for outstanding new plays and musicals. **116B**

Brooklyn Academy of Music (BAM)
@ Lafayette Av
@ Ashland Pl
36-4100
• America's oldest performing arts center, with four performance spaces offering imaginative and innovative music, dance and drama. **107D**

Brooklyn Center for the Performing Arts at Brooklyn College (BCBC)
Campus Rd @ Hillel Pl
51-4500
• World-class performing arts center presenting internationally acclaimed artists at affordable prices. **129A**

Brooklyn Philharmonic Orchestra
@ Lafayette Av
@ Ashland Pl
36-4137
• Innovative concert series and special events across Brooklyn. **107D**

Brooklyn Youth Chorus
138 Court St
243-9447
• Children's music education and concerts throughout Brooklyn. **107D**

Gowanus Arts Exchange
421 Fifth Av @ 8 St
832-0018
• Produces a varied family program of dance, theater, performance art and music year–round. **115A**

The Puppet Works
338 Sixth Av @ 4 St
965-3391
• Dedicated to the preservation and presentation of traditional marionette theatre. **115C**

651, An Arts Center
651 Fulton St
@ Hudson Av
636-4181
• Presents innovative and culturally diverse programs at Majestic Theater. **107D**

Thelma Hill Performing Arts Center
30 Third Av–Rm 602
(bet. Bergen & Dean Sts)
875-9710 **107C**

Zoos & Gardens

Coney Island NY Aquarium
W 8 St & Surf Av
265-FISH
• The nation's longest operating aquarium featuring over 10,000 specimens of sea life in naturalistic settings including an interactive children's exhibit. **143C**

Brooklyn Botanic Garden
1000 Washington Av
@ Empire Bd
622-4433
• New York City's premier plant kingdom, housing 12,000 varieties of flora. Famous for its rose, lilac and japanese gardens as well as the celebrity walk. **116C**

Prospect Park Wildlife Center
450 Flatbush Av
(off Empire Bd)
399-7339
• State-of-the-art children's zoo in Prospect Park that features seals, red pandas, and prairie dogs. Kids will enjoy the meerkats, and wallabies. **116C**

HISTORIC LANDMARKS

Bromelstein's Street Clock
Manhattan Av
(bet. Messerole and Norman Avs)
• Though Bromelstein's is gone, the clock is still running and one of a handful of street clocks left in NYC. Once chic advertisements, others can be found in the Rockaways and the Flatiron District. **102D**

Brooklyn Borough Hall
209 Joralemon St
• Built as Brooklyn's City Hall, here is the borough's oldest public building. Designed by Gamaliel King, this Greek Revival palace opened in 1851. The Victorian cupola was added in 1898. **108D**

Brooklyn Bridge
Downtown Brooklyn
(Cadman Plz)
• Designed by John A. Roebling. The world's longest suspension bridge of the 1900s, it took 16 years to build this span across the East River
(1867–1883). **107A**

Brooklyn Central Office, Bureau of Fire Communications
NYC Fire Department
35 Empire Bd
(near Prospect Park)
• This multi-use building was designed in Italian Renaissance style. **109C**

Brooklyn City Railroad Co Bldg
8 Cadman Plaza W
• In the age of the ferry boat, horse drawn carriages would line up here to bring passengers into the City of Brooklyn. Completed in 1861, this structure is a fine example of French Second Empire style. **108B**

Brooklyn College
2900 Bedford Av @
Av H, 951-5000
• Built by the Works Progress Administration (WPA) in the 1930s, Brooklyn College is located on a 26–acre campus, featuring a quadrangle flanked by Neo–Georgian buildings. **129A**

TO FIND A VENUE

Simply turn to page and locate the venue in grids A,B,C or D.

ATTRACTIONS

ATTRACTIONS

Brooklyn Heritage House
581 Mother Gaston Bd
385-1111 **118C**

Brooklyn Navy Yard
U.S. Naval Shipyard
Flushing Av
852-1441
• The nation's first Navy Yard (1801) housed 71,000 workers at the height of World War II. In the 1840s, the Federal–style Commandant's House (Quarters A at Hudson Av and Evans St), was home to Commodore Matthew Perry.
107B

Cadman Church
350 Clinton Av
@ President St
638-2231
• Founded in 1847 as the Clinton Avenue Congregational Church. The name changed in 1943 to honor Dr. S. Parkes Cadman, its distinguished pastor of 35 years. **114B**

Dime Savings Bank
9 DeKalb Av
(near the Gallery Mall at MetroTech)
• One of New York's greatest bank buildings boasting Ionic columns, ornate original furniture and an intricately cut marble floor.
109C

Eastern Parkway
Grand Army Plz to Ralph Av
• The nation's first parkway created by Olmstead and Vaux in 1866 as part of a regional system to bring open green spaces into the City. **116CD**

Eberhard-Faber Pencil Factory
61 Greenpoint Av
(bet. Franklin & West Sts)
• This alumnus of Greenpoint Manufacturing sports a façade made of pencils.
102A

Emmanuel Baptist Church
279 Lafayette Av
• The French 13th century Gothic–style church was completed in 1887. Its imposing twin tower design and triple arched entrance are constructed of Ohio sandstone. **110D**

Erasmus Hall Museum of Education
911 Flatbush Av
(near Church Av)
856-3571
• Built in 1786 as a private school for boys by the local Flatbush Dutch Reformed Church.
122B

Flatbush Dutch Reformed Church
890 Flatbush Av
@ Church Av
• Constructed (1793-1798) of Manhattan stone with Romanesque arched windows and doors, the building has a magnificent Georgian white wood tower. **122B**

Flatbush Town Hall
35 Snyder Av
(bet. Flatbush & Bedford Avs)
• Constructed in 1875 in the Victorian Gothic style, the former Town Hall served as a courthouse and a police station. **122D**

Flatlands Dutch Reformed Church
Kings Hwy @ E 40 St
• Constructed by Governor Stuyvesant, this Georgian/Federal church is one of the oldest (1848) Dutch parishes in the country. **129D**

Fort Hamilton Officers' Club
Whiting Quadrangle
Battery Av
• Located opposite Staten Island's Fort Wadsworth, this military granite fortification was built between 1825 and 1831 as part of the Totten system of seacoast forts. **134B**

George W. Wingate High School
600 Kingston Av
• Dedicated in 1955, this school resembles a banjo, with its circular shape and narrow wing design. **123A**

Greenpoint Savings Bank
Manhattan Av
@ Calyer St
• Known for its striking dome, the bank opened for business in 1863. **102D**

Greenwood Cemetery Gates
Fifth Av @ 25 St
788-7850
• This enormous 478–acre Victorian burial ground features a Greek revival main entrance gate. The gatehouse sports a clocktower and offices (1861). **121AB**

Hanson Place Seventh Day Adventist Church
88 Hanson Pl
@ Portland Av S
789-3030
• Originally known as Hanson Place Baptist Church when completed in 1860, this Greek Revival church features full length, paned windows of Victorian milk glass. **107D**

Lefferts Homestea
Flatbush Av
@ Empire Bd in Prospect Park
965-6505
• Built in 1783, the Dutch Colonial farmhouse moved to its resent site in 1918 and today is a children's historica museum with seasonal hours. **116**

Litchfield Villa
95 Prospect Park V
(bet. 4 & 5 Sts)
965-8900
Serving as the Brooklyn headqua ters of the NYC Parks Dept., the Italianate style mansion was built by Edwin C. Litchfie a prominent lawye and railroad magnate. **115**

The Magnolia Tree Earth Center
677 Lafayette Av
@ Tompkins Park
387-2116
• Brought from North Carolina in 1881, this bull bay magnolia (Magnol. grandiflora) bloom. every spring. Brooklyn's first Historic Living Landmark was established in 197 and serves as a focus for urban environmental programs. **11**

Ocean Parkway
Church to
Seabreeze Avs
• *Completed in 1876
to link Prospect Park
to Coney Island, this
grand avenue offers
tree-lined islands
for pedestrians and
a dedicated bike
path that follows
the length of the
parkway.* **128B–143B**

**Old Brooklyn Fire
Headquarters**
465-367 Jay St
• *Romanesque–
Revival style fire-
house built in the
late 1800s.* **109C**

**Old Gravesend
Cemetery**
Gravesend Neck Rd
& McDonald Av
• *This 1643 burial
ground for the Town
of Gravesend was
established by polit-
ical dissidents with
a charter that guar-
anteed the right of
conscience and
religious
freedom.* **136D**

The Parachute Jump
Boardwalk @ W 17
St (Steeplechase
Park site)
• *Formerly one of
the most famous of
rides at Coney
Island, it re-opened
at the 1939 World's
Fair at Flushing
Meadows.* **143C**

**Parsonage of Dutch
Reformed Church**
228 N 12 St
@ Driggs Av
• *This Romanesque
Revival style fire-
house is a well pre-
served example of
Frank Freeman's
architecture.* **102D**

**Russian Orthodox
Cathedral of the
Transfiguration**
228 N 12 St
@ Diggs Av
387-1064
• *Noted for the five
onion-domed cupo-
las, this 1921 cathe-
dral's interior fea-
tures a triple altar,
a central cupola
supported by four
columns and
period artwork.* **102D**

**St. Ann's &
the Holy Trinity
Church**
157 Montague St
@ Clinton St
875-6960
• *This Gothic Revival
style church has the
first American-
made stained glass
windows, recently
restored to their
former glory.* **108D**

**Salem Evangelical
Lutheran Church**
345 Ovington Av
@ 3 Av, 748-4024
• *The main feature
here is the naval
ship hanging from
the ceiling.* **126B**

**Soldiers' & Sailors'
Memorial Arch**
Grand Army Plz
• *Completed in 1892,
the monument com-
memorates Union
forces of the Civil
War. The arch sup-
ports a bas-relief
of Lincoln and
Grant.* **115B**

Steele House
200 Lafayette Av
• *The charming res-
idence of Joseph
Steele features
Greek Revival
clapboard design.
A federal style, two
story wing was
added in 1812. It
was sold in 1853 to
Joseph Brick, the
first president of the
Brooklyn Union Gas
Company.* **110D**

**Verrazano–
Narrows Bridge**
• *Soaring over the
Narrows between
Brooklyn and Staten
Island, it became the
largest single span
bridge in the world
in 1964.* **134A**

War Memorial
Cadman Plz &
Orange St
• *As the central part
of the Plaza's archi-
tecture, this memor-
ial completes an
intricate composi-
tion of terraces and
paths.* **108B**

**Weeksville Society
Hunterfly Road
Houses**
1968-1708 Bergen St
(bet. Rochester &
Buffalo Avs)
756-5250
• *The four small
frame houses recall
the days of Brooklyn's
first major African–
American Free
Settlement. Land pur-
chased by James
Week in 1838, was
later home to
Dr. Susan Smith
McKinney–Steward,
the first African–
American woman
physician in NY.* **117A**

**Williamsburg
Bank Building**
1 Hanson Place
@ Flatbush Av
• *Once Brooklyn's
tallest building, this
Byzantine structure
symbolizes Brooklyn's
financial institutions.
Built in 1929, the
tower sports the
world's highest four-
sided clock.* **107D**

Wyckoff House
5816 Clarendon Rd
@ Ralph Av
629-5400
• *Built by Pieter
Claeson Wyckoff in
1652, the oldest
house in NY offers
demonstrations of
wool spinning and
knitting in a 17th
century farm
setting.* **124C**

THEME PARKS

**Astroland
Amusement Park**
1000 Surf Av
372-0275
• *Premier amuse-
ment park and
home of the world
famous Cyclone
rollercoaster.* **143C**

**Deno's Wonder
Wheel Park**
305 W 12 St
@ Boardwalk
372-2592
• *18 kiddy rides and
five major thrill
rides including the
landmarked Wonder
Wheel. The adja-
cent Boardwalk is
one of the most
famous walkways in
the world, connect-
ing Brighton Beach
to Coney Island.*
143C

FunTime USA
2461 Knapp St,
368-0500
• *NYC's largest
indoor family
entertainment
center.* **143C**

**Nellie Bly
Amusement Park**
1824 Shore Pkwy
996-4002
• *Fun for the whole
family– a favorite
Brooklyn
destination.* **143C**

ATTRACTIONS

BANKS & FINANCIAL SERVICES

Astoria Federal Savings Bank & Loan
1 Astoria Federal Plz, QS, 516-327-7575

Atlantic Bank of New York
960 Sixth Av, MA
212-695-5400

Atlantic Liberty Savings Federal Association
186 Montague St
855-3555 **108D**

Banco Popular de Puerto Rico
166 Livingston St
596-1351 **109C**

Banco Popular de Puerto Rico
918 Seneca Av in Ridgewood, QS
718-417-7878

Carver Federal Savings Bank
1281 Fulton St
@ Nostrand Av
783-4506 **116B**

Central Brooklyn Federal Credit Union
1205 Fulton St
@ Bedford Av
399-1763 **116A**

Chase Manhattan Bank
1 Pierrepont Plz
800-242-7324 **108D**

Citibank, NA
1 Court Sq
Long Island City, QS
627-3999

Community Capital Bank
111 Livingston St
802-1212 **108D**

Cross County Federal Savings Bank
731 Metropolitan Av
388-4400

The Dime Savings Bank of New York
9 DeKalb Av
234-9992 **109C**

The Dime Savings Bank of Williamsburgh
1902 Kings Hwy
336-1300 **130A**

EAB
195 Montague St
895-3404 **108D**

Flatbush Federal Savings & Loan
2146 Nostrand Av
859-6800 **108D**

Fleet Bank, NA
300 Cadman Plz W
800-331-9994 **108D**

Flushing Savings Bank
7102 Third Av @ 71 St, 836-8088 **126B**

Greenpoint Bank
356 Fulton St
800-554-7336 **108D**

Independence Community Bank
195 Montague St
722-5300 or
800-732-3434 **108D**

Branches:
• 6424 18 Av
@ 65 St
259-5100 **127D**

• 130 Court St
@ Atlantic Av
722-5700 **108D**

• 23 Newkirk Plz
(in Newkirk Plz Shopping Center)
@ 18 Av,
859-8888 **128B**

• 1769 86 St
@ Eighteenth Av
236-4400 **135A**

• 2357-59 86 St
(bet. 23 & 24 Av)
946-8144 **135D**

• 4514 Sixteenth Av
@ 45 St
972-8370 **128A**

• 440 Av P
(bet. E 2 & E 3 Sts)
627-8387 **136B**

• 1310 Kings Hwy
(bet. E 13 & E 14 Sts)
998-6767 **137A**

• 301 Av U
@ McDonald Av
946-0900 **136D**

• 7500 Fifth Av
@ Bay Ridge Pkwy
745-6100 **126B**

• 8808 Fifth Av
(bet. 88 & 89 St)
833-4240 **126D**

• 200 Willoughby Av
(on campus of Pratt Institute)
636-3886 **110D**

• 234 Prospect Park W (bet. Windsor Pl & Prospect Av)
499-0947 **115C**

• 195 Montague St
(bet. Court & Clinton Sts)
722-5650 **108D**

• 1302 Av J
(bet E 13 & E 14 Sts)
258-1004 **128D**

• 4823 Thirteenth Av
@ 49 St
633-8000 **128A**

498 Columbia St
@ Lorraine St
797-0323 **114A**

M & T Bank
7807 Fifth Av
800-724-2440 **126D**

Marine Midland Bank
188 Montague St
800-627-4631 **108D**

New York Federal Savings Bank
2 Park Av, MA
212-779-2700

Ponce De Leon Federal Savings
169 Smith St
852-9500 **109C**

Republic National Bank of New York
1 Hanson Pl
@ intersection of Flatbush & Atlantic Avs, 488-4050 **107D**

Richmond County Savings Bank
4523 Amboy Rd, SI
984-2378

Ridgewood Savings Bank
71-02 Forest Av
Ridgewood, QS
240-4800

Staten Island Savings Bank
9512 Third Av
447-8880 **126C**

BUSINESS SERVICE ORGANIZATIONS

Belmont Merchants Association
29 Belmont Av
345-8877
• Serves Belmont Av in the Brownsville community.

Brighton Beach BID
1002 Brighton Beach Av, 934-1908
• Serves Brighton Beach Av from Ocean Pkwy to Brighton 15 St.

Brooklyn Chamber of Commerce
7 MetroTech Center
875-1000
• Business services and economic development throughout Brooklyn.

Brooklyn Economic Development Corp.
30 Flatbush Av
522-4600
• Serves businesses around the borough.

Brooklyn Neighborhood Improvement Association Inc.
1482 St. John's Pl
Suite 1F, 773-4116
• Serves Prospect Heights, Clinton Hill and West Crown Heights.

Caribbean American Chamber of Commerce
26 Brooklyn Navy Yard, 834-4544
• Serves Brooklyn's business community.

Church Av BID
1720 Church Av, 2 Flr
287-2600
• Serves Flatbush from 16 St to Coney Island Av.

Coney Island Board of Trade
1505 Mermaid Av
373-9600
• Serves the community of Coney Island.

East Williamsburg Valley Industrial Development Corp.
11-29 Catherine St
388-7287

Flatbush Av BID
1033 Flatbush Av
941-3914
• Serves the Flatbush community from Parkside Av to Cortelyou Rd.

Fulton Mall Improvement Assoc.
356 Fulton St
852-5118
• Serves Fulton St from Adams St to Flatbush Av.

Grand St BID
11-29 Catherine St,
3 flr, 388-5454 ext.169
• Serves Grand Av between Bushwick and Union Avs.

Kings Highway BID
1628 Kings Hwy
645-1100
• Serves Kings Hwy and Quentin Rd.

LDC of Broadway
911 Broadway
574-8917
• Serves Broadway bet. Rodney St and Myrtle Av.

LDC of East New York
116 Williams Av
385-6700
• Serves New Lots Av in East New York and Brownsville.

Midwood Development Corp.
1416 Av M
376-0999
• Serves Midwood.

Neighbors Helping Neighbors
5323 Fifth Av, 2 Flr
492-3450
• Serves Prospect Park W/Kensington.

New Perspectives
77 Conklin Av
272-3887
• Serves Canarsie along Av L.

North Brooklyn Development Corp.
894 Manhattan Av
389-9044
• Serves Greenpoint community.

North Flatbush BID
346 Flatbush Av
783-1685
• Serves Flatbush Av from Atlantic Av to St. John's Pl.

Nostrand Av Business Assoc.
718 Nostrand Av
493-8322
• Serves Nostrand Av from Atlantic Av to Eastern Pkwy in Crown Heights.

MetroTech BID
4 MetroTech Center
488-8200
• Serves MetroTech/Downtown Brooklyn.

OBUSTY
1079 Gates Av
452-6150
• Serving Oceanhill, Bushwick and Bedford–Stuyvesant communities.

Pitkin Av BID
1572 Pitkin Av
922-2466
• Serves Pitkin and Rockaway Avenues in Brownsville.

Ralph Av Merchants Association
132 Ralph Av
453-9490
• Serves Bushwick on Ralph Av from Quincy St to Atlantic Av.

South Brooklyn Local Development Corporation
269 Van Brunt St
625-8624
• Serves South Brooklyn and Red Hook.

Sunset Park– Fifth Av BID
4505 Fifth Av
437-2234
• Serves Fifth Av from 38 to 64 St in Sunset Park.

Washington Av Merchants Association
840 Washington Av
636-4685
• Serves Washington Av from Park Pl to Eastern Pkwy.

Woodhull Community BID
39 Graham Av
387-6643
• Serves Graham Av, Cook St and Broadway.

DINING

CATERING HALLS

Bay Ridge Manor
476 76 St
748-8855
• *Classic catering hall in the heart of Bay Ridge.* **126B**

El Caribe Country Club
5945 Strickland Av
531-1200
• *Superior food, classy decor at this huge Mill Basin favorite.* **130D**

Grand Prospect Hall
263 Prospect Av
788-0777
• *They make your dreams come true here.* **122A**

Polonaise Terrace Caterers
150 Greenpoint Av,
383-3700
• *There's no scrimping on the food at this Greenpoint gem.* **102B**

ABBREVIATIONS

(M) = Closed Mon.
(T) = Closed Tue.
(S) = Closed Sun.
(SS) = Closed Sat. & Sun.
(R) = Reservations required
(CO) = Cash Only

BROOKLYN EATS

For detailed reviews of Brooklyn's Best restaurants, pick-up a copy of "Brooklyn Eats" at your local bookstore

DINING

Abbracciamento on the Pier *SS*
2200 Rockaway Pkwy @ the Canarsie Pier
251-5517, Valet and lot parking.
• *Northern Italian with views of Jamaica Bay.* **131B**

Acadia Parish Cajun Café *S*
148 Atlantic Av
(bet Clinton & Henry Sts), 624-5154 (T)
• *Cajun cuisine with real Louisiana charm.* **108C**

Adelman's *S*
1906 Kings Hwy
(bet. E 19 & Ocean Av), 336-4915
• *Real, old–fashioned deli.* **137A**

Aiello's *S*
1406 Neptune Av
@ Stillwell Av
373-1155
• *Great Italian in the shadow of Coney Island.* **143C**

Baci *S*
7107 Third Av
(bet. 71 St & Ovington Av)
836-5536 (M)
• *Spanish bistro.* **126B**

Amin Indian Cuisine *S*
140 Montague St
(bet. Clinton & Henry Sts) 855-4791
• *Indian restaurant in the heart of Brooklyn Heights.* **108D**

Areo *SS*
8424 Third Av @ 85 St, 238-0079 (M)
• *Italian fare served in elegant Romanesque rooms.* **126C**

Arirang Hibachi Steakhouse *SS*
8814 Fourth Av
(bet. 88 & 89 Sts)
238-9880
• *Japanese food in an authentic atmosphere that is entertaining, especially for kids.* **126D**

Armando's *SS*
143 Montague St
(bet. Henry & Clinton Sts)
624-7167
• *Traditional Italian fare at one of Montague Streets oldest restaurants.* **108D**

Aunt Suzie's Kitchen *S*
247 Fifth Av (bet. Garfield Pl & Carroll St), 788-3377
• *Homey setting with old Italian family favorites.* **115A**

Bamonte's *SS*
32 Withers St
(bet. Lorimer & Union Sts)
384-8831 (T)
• *Festive family favorite in the heart of Williamsburg.* **104D**

Bangkok Thai House *S*
6735 Third Av
(bet. Senator & 68 Sts)
748-9354 (CO)
• *Cozy, candlelit Thai.* **126B**

Bay Plaza *SS*
2801 Emmons Av @ E 28 St
769-7100 (R)
• *Enjoy the seafood at this Sheepshead Bay Italian.* **144B**

Bean *S*
167 Bedford Av @ N 8 St
387-8222 (CO)
• *Mexican restaurant favored by the Williamsburg artist set.* **104B**

Bon Appetit *S*
2919 Av S @ Nostrand Av
382-4500 (R)
• *Lively Italian kitchen in Marine Park.* **137B**

Brawta *S*
347 Atlantic Av @ Hoyt St
855-5515
• *Represents the coming of age of West Indian restaurants.* **107**

Brennan & Carr *S*
3432 Nostrand Av @ Av U, 769-1254
• *Best thinly sliced roast beef sandwiches in the universe at this American classic.* **137**

Buckley's *SS*
2926 Av S @ Nostrand Av
998-4222
• *Basic American food with Italian, German and French influenced items.* **137**

Café Carciofo *S*
248 Court St @ Kane St
624-7551 (CO)
• *Charming Italian café in the heart of Cobble Hill.* **107**

Café Love *S*
215 Court St @ Warren St
875-4568
• *Truly a vegetarian's delight.* **107**

afé St. Petersburg
223 Brighton
each Av
et. Brighton 1 &
righton 2)
3-0880 (R)
*Small, quiet
ussian restaurant
/ Brighton Beach
andards.* **144C**

affe Buon Gusto *$*
1 Montague St
et. Clinton &
enry Sts, 624-3838
*Friendly neighbor-
ood Italian in the
eart of Brooklyn
eights.* **108D**

affe Roma *$*
01 Stillwell Av
Av T, 372-4550 (M)
*Come for the schi-
cciatas–freshly
aked bread with
yers of filling
aked inside.* **136C**

ambodian Cuisine
37 S Elliott Pl
et. Lafayette Av
Fulton St)
8-3262 (CO)
*An adventurous
aters dream: good,
expensive and
ique.* **110C**

nedos *$$*
16 Third Av
et. 73 & 74 Sts)
8-1908
*Northern Italian
od graciously
erved.* **126B**

Caravan *$*
193 Atlantic Av
(near Court St)
488-7111 (R)
*Yemenite restau-
rant with emphasis
on native
cuisine.* **107C**

**Carolina Country
Kitchen** *$*
1993 Atlantic Av
@ Saratoga Av
346-4400 (CO)
*Southern cooking
served cafeteria–
style.* **117B**

Casa Pepe *$$*
114 Bay Ridge Av
@ Colonial Rd
833-8865
*Haven for Spanish
cuisine.* **126A**

Casa Rosa *$*
384 Court St
@ Carroll St
625-8874 (M)
*Quality Italian
food.* **107C**

Casey's Café *$*
2 MetroTech Center,
624-0200 (SS)
*Traditional
American and
Italian dishes.* **109C**

Castle Harbour *$$*
3149 Emmons Av
@ Coyle St
332-0046
*A vast menu from
pasta to steak and
chicken, but come
for the fish.* **145A**

Chadwick's *$$*
8822 Third Av
(bet. 88 & 89 Sts)
833-9855
*A real gem on Bay
Ridge's Restaurant
Row.* **126C**

Chef Wong Seafood
$ 2170 86 St
@ Bay Pkwy
373-9122
*This Bensonhurst
Chinese restaurant
has a lot to offer.* **135D**

Chianti *$*
8530 Third Av
@ 85 St, 921-6300
*A place meant
for romance.* **126D**

Christina's *$*
853 Manhattan Av
@ Noble St
383-4382 (CO)
*Homemade,
inexpensive
Polish food.* **102B**

Cino's *$$*
243 DeKalb Av
(bet. Vanderbilt &
Clermont Avs)
622-9249 (S)
*Americanized
Italian cuisine at
this neighborhood
institution.* **110C**

Circles Canteena *$*
8001 Fifth Av
@ 80 St, 745-9160
*Hang out at this
relaxing Mexican
cantina.* **126D**

Circles Grill *$*
9023 Third Av
(bet. 90 & 91 Sts)
748-7470
*Enjoy exotic
cuisines of many
worlds.* **126C**

Coco Reef *$$*
222 Seventh Av
@ 3 St, 788-5036
*Feast on sizzling
black peppercorn
beef and other
divine Malaysian
and Singaporan
treats.* **115C**

Coco Roco *$*
392 Fifth Av
(bet. 6 & 7 Sts)
965-3376
*Colorful Peruvian
restaurant serving
delectable rotisserie
chicken.* **115C**

**Cono and Sons
O'Pescatore** *$$*
301 Graham Av
@ Ainslie St
388-0168
*Special for fish and
other delights of the
sea.* **104B**

**Continental
Ristorante** *$*
395 Bridge St
(bet. Willoughby St
& Fulton Mall)
624-9636
*Hearty Italian
served cafeteria–
style. Lunch only.* **104B**

Corn Bread Café *$*
434 Seventh Av
(bet. 14 & 15 Sts)
768-3838
*A new home for
Southern food in
Park Slope.* **115C**

Cucina *$$*
256 Fifth Av
(bet. Garfield Pl &
Carroll St)
230-0711 (M)
*Tuscan–style
Italian in Park Slope
owned and operat-
ed by Brooklyn's
most famous chef,
Michael Ayoub.* **115A**

Dario's *$*
9824 Fourth Av
@ 98 St, 836-0378
*Wonderful,
romantic little Italian
restaurant.* **134A**

Diner *$*
85 Broadway
@ Berry St
486-3077
*Bisto fare served
to a young artist
crowd at this 1920's
retired, real dining
car.* **104A**

**Edna's Glatt Kosher
Delicatessen** *$*
125 Church Av
@ McDonald Av
438-8207,
800-924-5533
*Special lunch
and dinner is
served.* **122C**

DINING

Eamonn Doran $$
174 Montague St
(near Court St)
596-4969
• Small selection of
Irish pub special-
ties, but the menu
primarily nods to
the French. **108D**

Empire China $
815 Av U
(bet. E 8 & 9 St)
336-8068
• Chinese food,
modern decor
and courteous
service. **136C**

**Einstein Bros.
Bagels** $
2 MetroTech Center
@ Myrtle Av
246-4620
• Overstuffed
sandwiches on
fresh bagels. **109C**

Embers $$
9519 Third Av
(bet. 95 & 96 Sts)
745-3700 (CO)
Valet Parking
• Come for big, juicy
cuts of steak. Try
the 60 ounce T-bone
for two. **126C**

ABBREVIATIONS

(M) = Closed Mon.
(T) = Closed Tue.
(S) = Closed Sun.
(SS) = Closed Sat.
       & Sun.
(R) = Reservations
       required
(CO) = Cash Only

Fitzpatrick's Café $
8622 Third Av
(bet. 86 & 87 Sts)
680-7862
• Great pub grub in
a bistro atmos-
phere. **126C**

Fontana Bella $$
2086 Coney Island
Av @ Kings Hwy
627-3904
• Kosher Italian,
Mediterranean gem
in the heart of
Midwood. **136B**

The Fountain $
183 Atlantic Av
(bet. Court & Clinton
Sts)
624-6764
• Middle Eastern
fare, clean white
decor. **107C**

Frost $$
193 Frost St
@ Humbolt St
389-3347 (M)
• Wonderful Sicilian
family Italian
restaurant. **102D**

Fujisan $
7419 Third Av
(bet. 74th St &
Bay Ridge Pkwy)
238-3444
• All the dainty
details are attended
to at this fresh sushi
spot. **126B**

Fujisan $
161 Seventh Av
(bet. 1 St and
Garfield Pl)
768-3976
• All the dainty
details are attended
to at this fresh sushi
spot. **115A**

Fujisan $$
130 Montague St
@ Henry St
858-8077
• Try this quaint
Height's spot for
people watching
and sushi. **108D**

Gage & Tollner $$$
372 Fulton St
(bet. Jay St & Elm Pl)
875-5181
• First rate food
and service at
this Brooklyn
landmark. **108D**

Gargiulo's $$
2911 West 15 St
(bet. Surf &
Mermaid Avs)
266-4891 (T)
• Fantastic food
from an extensive
Neapolitan
menu. **143C**

Geido $
331 Flatbush Av
@ Seventh Av
638-8866 (M)
• Distinctly Japanese
restaurant with
fresh sushi served
in a matter-of-fact
manner. **115B**

Gia Lam $
5402 Eighth Av
@ 54 St
854-8818 (CO)
• Popular
Vietnamese in
Brooklyn's Chinatown.
121C

Giando on the Water
$$ 400 Kent Av
@ Broadway
387-7000 (R)
• Tasty Italian and a
spectacular view of
the Manhattan
skyline. **104C**

Goodfella's $
9606 Third Av
@ 96 St, 833-6200
• Atmosphere
and food satisfies
both children and
adults **134A**

**Greenhouse
Café** $$
7717 Third Av
@ 77 St
833-8200
• Vegetarians
and carnivores
are happy at this
Bay Ridge
mainstay. **126B**

**Griswold's Pub
& Restaurant** $$
7726 Third Av
@ 77 St
745-3340
• Tasty American
establishment. **126B**

Grotta D'Oro $$$
3206 Emmons Av
@ Knapp St
646-4300 (R)
• Fine Italian
cuisine just steps
from Sheepshead
Bay. **145A**

Halcyon $
227 Smith
@ Butler St
260-WAXY
• Espresso, cakey
treats and fresh
house music serve
all day at this cozy
pad in Cobble Hill.
106C

Harvest $
218 Court St
(bet. Baltic & Warre
Sts)
624-9267 (M)
• Down home feel
ing and Southern-
style cooking. **10**

**Healthy
Henrietta's** $
60 Henry St
(bet. Orange &
Cranberry Sts)
858-8478
• Wonderful, unpr.
tentious vegetaria
delight in Brooklyn
Heights. **10**

**Healthy Henrietta
on the Slope** $
787 Union St
(bet. Fifth &
Sixth Avs)
622-2924
• More wonders a
the Park Slope
location. **11**

Hamilton House $
10033 Fourth Av
@ 101 St
745-9090 (R)
• Teriffic steak. **13**

DINING

Heights Café *$$*
84 Montague St
@ Hicks St
625-5555
• *Sophisticated,
contemporary bistro
in Brooklyn Heights.*
108C

Henry's End *$$*
44 Henry St
(bet. Middagh &
Cranberry Sts)
834-1776
• *Warm, neighbor-
hood feel with great
food and
service.* **108**B

**Hokkaido
Japanese** *$$*
9326 Fourth Av
@ 93 St
680-3917
• *Very beautiful,
very Japanese.* **126**C

**Hunter's Steak &
Ale House** *$*
9404 Fourth Av
(bet. 94 & 95 Sts)
238-8899
• *Hearty steaks and
an extensive beer
selection.* **126**D

Inaka *$*
225 Seventh Av
@ Fourth St
499-7856
• *Solid Japanese
food and creative
sushi in Park
Slope.* **115**C

Inaka *$*
158 Court St
(bet. Amity &
Pacific Sts)
797-2888
• *Lovely Japanese
presentation and
great service.* **107**C

India Passage *$$*
7407 Third Av
@ 74 St
833-2160
• *Tasty Indian cui-
sine and gracious
service.* **126**B

International *$$*
4408 Fifth Av
(bet. 44 & 45 Sts)
438-2009
• *Puerto Rican and
Dominican restau-
rant at Brooklyn's
industrial core.* **120**B

Jade Plaza *$*
6022 Eighth Av
@ 60 St
492-6888
• *Hong Kong and
Cantonese specials
in Sunset Park
Chinatown.* **121**C

Johnny Mack's *$*
1114 Eighth Av
(bet. 11 & 12 Sts)
832-7961
• *American comfort
food and great juke-
box at cozy neigh-
borhood joint.* **115**C

Joloff *$*
930 Fulton St
@ St James Pl
636-4011 (CO)
• *Simple, home-
style Senegalese
cooking and color-
ful, Afro–centric
decor.* **110**D

Junior's *$$*
386 Flatbush Av
@ DeKalb Av
852-5257
• *#1 Cheesecake
in New York, but
there's also an
extensive deli
menu.* **109**C

Kalio *$$*
254 Court St @ Kane
St, 625-1295 (M)
• *New American:
fresh and lively
cuisine.* **107**C

Kar *$*
5908 Av N
(bet. E 59 St &
Ralph Av) 531-8811
• *Innovative
Chinese
cuisine. Try the
eight wonder soup,
a little bit of every-
thing.* **130**D

Kasia's *$*
146 Bedford Av
@ N 9 St
387-8780 (SS)
• *Neighborhood
artists flock here
for Polish diner
food.* **104**B

Keur N' Deye *$*
737 Fulton St
(bet. S Elliott &
S Portland Sts)
875-4937 (CO) (M)
• *Traditional
Senegalese home
cooking and
African-inspired
decor.* **110**C

La Bouillabaisse *$*
145 Atlantic Av
(bet. Henry & Clinton
Sts)
522-8275 (CO)
• *So French, and yet
so Brooklyn. Come
with an appetite.*
108D

La Trattoria *$*
2811 Av U
(bet. E 28 & E 29 Sts)
648-0334 (T)
• *Classic Italian–
American.* **137**D

La Traviata *$*
139 Montague St
(bet. Clinton &
Henry Sts)
858-4100
• *Italian eatery
serving up pizza
and traditional
Sicilian fare.* **108**D

La Villita *$*
1249 Av U @ E 13 St
998-0222
• *Spanish menu
in Sheepshead
Bay.* **137**C

Laila *$*
440 Seventh Av
@ 15 St, 788-0268
• *Middle Eastern
home cooking.* **115**C

Las Tres Palmas *$*
124 Court St
(bet. Atlantic Av &
State St) 624-9565
• *Great Spanish
food in a simple set-
ting.* **108**D

**Laura's Gourmet
Kitchen** *$*
1235 Prospect Av
@ Reeves Pl
436-3715
• *Expansive Italian
menu in an elegant
setting.* **122**A

**Le Bistro Bar &
Restaurant** *$$*
279 Flatbush Av
(bet. St Marks &
Prospect Places)
399-2000
• *West Indian and
American cuisine in
a quiet, formal din-
ing room.* **115**B

Le Gamin Café *$*
1 Main St @ East
River, 399-7100
• *French bistro fare
with Manhattan
skyline and
Brooklyn Bridge
views. Live music
accompanies the
Sunday brunch.*
107A

PRICE KEY

Prices given
include average
cost of a dinner
and an alcoholic
beverage without
tax and tip.

$ = $5-$20
$$ = $21-$35
$$$ = $36-$55
$$$$ = Over $55

DINING

Lemongrass Grill *S*
61A Seventh Av
(bet. Lincoln &
Berkeley Pl)
399-7100
• *Disney Thai dining
experience.* **115A**

**Lentos of
Park Slope** *S*
833 Union St
(bet. Sixth &
Seventh Avs)
399-8782
• *Solid Italian menu
in a former carriage
house.* **115A**

**Lily's Public
House** *SS*
8814 Third Av
@ 88 St
833-6466
• *Dark paneling,
roaring fire and
quality menu.* **126C**

Los Mariachis *S*
805 Coney Island Av
@ Cortelyou Rd
826-3388
• *Authentic
Mexican with a
festive and cheery
atmosphere.* **128B**

Louise's *S*
54 Rockaway Av
(bet. Marion St
& Broadway)
574-7514
(M) (CO)
• *Cafeteria-style
West Indian
cuisine.* **112C**

lucian bleu *SS*
63 Lafayette Av
@ Fulton St
422-0093
• *Modern American
cuisine with multi-
ethnic influences.
Enjoy the outdoor
garden and live
music on Fridays.* **107D**

Lundy's *SS*
1901 Emmons Av
@ Ocean Av
743-0022
• *Fresh seafood at
the legendary
Lundy's.* **144B**

Mama Tury *SS*
1652 86 St
@ 16 Av
256-8905 (M)
• *Very homemade
Northern Italian cui-
sine.* **135A**

Mambo Italiano *SS*
8803 Third Av
(bet. 88 & 89 Sts)
833-3891
• *Live music,
funky atmosphere,
like an Italian
neighborhood
block party.* **126C**

Marco Polo *SS*
345 Court St
@ Union St
852-5015
• *An Italian delight
for locals and
visitors alike in the
heart of Carroll
Gardens.* **114B**

**Mario and Luigi's
Seafood & Pasta Grill**
SS 2007 Emmons Av
(bet. Ocean Av &
Sheepshead Bay Rd)
891-4300
• *Brightly lit Italian
that's just plain
fun.* **144B**

Max & Moritz *SS*
428 Seventh Av (bet.
14 & 15 Sts)
499-5557
• *Contemporary
American and
French Cuisine.* **115C**

Meson Flamenco *SS*
135 Atlantic Av
(bet. Henry &
Clinton Sts)
625-7177
• *Complete Spanish
food experience
and live Flamenco
on weekends.* **108C**

Metro Star Café *S*
369 Jay St
(near Willoughby St)
852-5892
• *Italian specialties
and sandwiches
served cafeteria–
style.* **108D**

Mezcal's *S*
151 Atlantic Av
(bet. Clinton &
Henry Sts)
643-6000
• *Mexican eatery
known for its
appetizers.* **108C**

Mezzanotte *SS*
8408 Third Av
(bet. 84 & 85 Sts)
238-5000 (M)
• *Minimalist,
upscale dining
experience in Bay
Ridge.* **126D**

Michael's *SS*
2929 Av R
@ Nostrand Av
998-7851
• *Sophisticated,
Italian palate for
better-informed
diners.* **137B**

Mike & Tony's *SS*
239 Fifth Av
@ Carroll St
857-2800
• *Cigar bar, great
food, and old world
ambiance.* **115A**

Mike's International
S 552 Flatbush Av
(bet. Lincoln &
Maple Sts)
856-7034
• *Real Jamaican
fare with
simple, elegant
ambiance.* **116C**

Miss Ann's *S*
86 S Portland Av
(bet. Fulton St &
Lafayette Av)
858-6997 (SMT) (CO)
• *Southern–style
cooking rules at this
tiny, storefront
restaurant.* **107D**

**Montague
Street Saloon** *S*
122 Montague St
(bet. Henry & Hicks
Sts) 522-6770
• *Fast service and
top-of-the-line bar
food.* **108D**

Moroccan Star *S*
205 Atlantic Av
(bet. Court & Clinton
Sts) 643-0800
• *Standout
Middle Eastern
cuisine.* **108D**

Nam *S*
222 Seventh Av
@ 3 St, 788-5036
• *Very chic
Vietnamese with
an extensive
menu.* **115A**

National *SSS*
273 Brighton Beach
Av @ Brighton
Second St
646-1225 (R)
• *Dancing, a floor
show, and portions
the size of Mother
Russia.* **144C**

New City Café *SS*
246 DeKalb Av
(bet. Vanderbilt &
Clermont Avs)
622-5607
• *Contemporary
American with a
definite French
twist.* **110C**

New Corner *$$*
201 Eighth Av
@ 72 St
33-0800
• *Broad range of
Italian fare has kept
three generations of
diners coming back.*
26D

New Mexicali *$*
37 Court St
@ Atlantic Av
25-7370
• *Fresh Tex–Mex
with an innovative
air.* **107C**

New Prospect Café *$*
393 Flatbush Av
Eighth Av &
Sterling Pl)
88-2148
• *An American
favorite on the Park
Slope scene.* **115C**

New Ruan's *$$*
955 86 St
bet. 19 & 20 Avs)
66-8888
• *Well above
average Chinese
cooking.* **135B**

Nino's *$$*
973 Coney Island Av
bet. Av P & Quentin
d) 336-7872
• *Southern Italian
is an understated
and sophisticated
setting.* **136B**

Nino's *$$*
215 Union St
(bet. Clinton &
Henry Sts)
858-5370
• *Generous
portions in a
cheery and open
atmosphere.* **114B**

Noodle Pudding *$$*
38 Henry St
(bet. Cranberry &
Middagh Sts)
625-3737 (M) (CO)
• *Warm ambiance
and offers both
Northern and
Southern Italian
specialties.* **108B**

Nordic *$$*
6925 Third Av
@ 69 St
745-3939 (M)
• *Scandinavian
restaurant in
the heart of Bay
Ridge.* **126B**

Northside Café *$*
119 Kent Av
388-9000
• *Neighborhood
Italian with a rowdy
bar.* **102C**

Ocean Palace *$$*
5423 Eighth Av
@ 54 St, 871-8080
• *The emperor
of Brooklyn's
Chinatown.* **121C**

Odessa *$$*
1113 Brighton Beach
Av
(bet. Brighton 13 &
14 Sts)
332-3223 (R)
• *The remodeled
Odessa is a little
more sedate as
Russian nightclubs
go. Come for the
music, Russian
food and vodka.* **144D**

Off Shore *$*
7822 Third Av
@ 78 St
921-5900 (CO)
• *Small, cozy and
private, the home
cooked fare ranges
from burgers to full
course meals.* **126B**

101 *$$*
10018 Fourth Av
@ 101 St, 833-1313
• *Art deco bistro in
the shadow of the
Verazzano Narrows
Bridge.* **134A**

Ortobello *$*
6401 Bay Pkwy
@ 64 St, 236-9810
• *Rich selection of
traditional Southern
Italian fare with all
the extras.* **136A**

Oznots Dish *$*
79 Berry St
@ N 9 St, 599-6596
• *Creative Mediter-
ranean fair in a
bistro setting.* **102C**

Park Plaza *$$*
220 Cadman Plz W
@ Pineapple St
596-5900
• *Upscale diner
overlooking
Cadman Plaza
Park.* **108B**

**Park Slope
Brewing Company** *$*
356 Sixth Av
@ 5 St
788-1756
• *Brew pub with an
eclectic menu.* **115C**

Patois *$$*
255 Smith St
(bet. Douglas &
Degraw Sts)
855-1535
• *The G-spot of
French cooking on
Smith Street where
the mustard crusted
lamb chops are
divine.* **114B**

Pearl Room *$$*
8203 Third Av
@ 82 St
833-6666
• *American menu
with emphasis on
fresh ingredients
and seafood.* **126D**

Pete's Downtown
$$ One Old Fulton St
@ Water St
858-3510 (M)
• *Mostly Italian just
steps away from
the waterfront.* **107A**

**Peter Luger
Steakhouse** *$$$*
178 Broadway
(bet. Bedford &
Briggs Avs)
387-0500 (CO) (R)
• *Legendary
steaks, hand–
picked and aged
on the premises
served in a
German beer
hall–type
atmosphere.* **104A**

Pho Hoai *$*
1906 Av U
(bet. E 18 & E 19 Sts)
616-1233 (CO)
• *Spare and casual,
but distinctly
Vietnamese.* **137C**

Pino's Pasta Café *$*
3338 Nostrand Av
(bet. Avs S & T)
645-7700 (CO)
• *Very simple, won-
derful full-service
café.* **137B**

Plan Eat Thailand *$*
141 N 7 St
@ Berry St
599-5758 (CO)
• *Delightful Thai is a
staple in Williams-
burg's jumping artist
neighborhood.* **104B**

Polonica *$*
7214 Third Av
(bet. 72 & 73 Sts)
630-5805 (CO)
• *Polish fare on Bay
Ridge's restaurant
Row* **126B**

PRICE KEY

Prices given
include average
cost of a dinner
and an alcoholic
beverage without
tax and tip.

$ = $5-$20
$$ = $21-$35
$$$ = $36-$55
$$$$ = Over $55

DINING

Ponte Vecchio *SS*
8810 Fourth Av
(bet. 88 & 89 Sts)
238-6449
• Good solid Italian
fare coupled with
good service. **126**D

**Prima Pasta
& Café** *S*
9110 Fourth Av (bet.
91 & 92 Sts)
833-4700
• Mouth-watering
desserts at this
pasta café. **126**D

Primorski *S*
282 Brighton Beach
Av @ Brighton 3
891-3111 (CO)
• Disco never
died in Brighton
Beach– enjoy the
Georgian food and
dancing. **144**C

Queen *SSS*
84 Court St
596-5954 (CO)
• Old-time down-
town favorite (politi-
cians and judges
love it) that will put
you in an Italian
state of mind. **108**D

Randazzo's Clam Bar
S 2017 Emmons Av
(bet. Ocean Av
& E 21 St)
615-0010 (CO)
• Come for the
clams and oysters
by the dozens. **144**B

Rasputin *SS*
2670 Coney Island Av
@ Av X
332-8111 (R)
• Russian nightclub
with Vegas–style
entertainment. **144**A

Red Rose *S*
315 Smith St
(bet. President &
Union Sts)
625-0963 (T)
• Small, family
Italian restaurant
with everything
from fresh pasta
to pizza. **114**B

Red's Italian *S*
3712 Thirteenth Av
@ 37 St
436-1818 (M)
• Traditional Italian
menu from pasta to
veal with huge
portions. **121**D

Richard Yee's *SS*
2617-19 Av U
(bet. E 26 & 27 Sts)
891-9090
• Dark, romantic
Chinese with a
hot, jazzy 1970s
look. **137**D

River Café *SSSS*
One Water St
522-5200
• No jeans; jacket
required for men.
Exciting cuisine
with a spectacular
view of Downtown
Manhattan. **107**A

Romano *SS*
7117 13 Av
(bet. 71 & 72 Sts)
232-5226
• Old-time
family Italian
restaurant. **127**C

St. Michel *SS*
7518 Third Av
(bet. 75 and 76 Sts)
748-4411 (M)
• Sophisticated
room, efficient
service and very
French. **102**D

Sahara *S*
2337 Coney Island Av
(bet. Avs U &T)
376-8594
• Delightful Turkish
cuisine and a casu-
al atmosphere. **137**C

Sancho's *SS*
7410 Third Av
(bet. 74 & 75 Sts)
748-0770
• Traditional
Spanish restaurant
with a dark, inti-
mate interior. **126**B

Santa Fe Grill *S*
62 Seventh Av
@ Lincoln Pl
636-0279
• Southwestern
cuisine in this
relaxed, neighbor-
hood joint. **115**B

Sapodilla Café *S*
412 Myrtle Av
(bet. Clinton &
Vanderbilt Avs)
797-1213
• Everything
for Southern
or Caribbean
palates. **110**C

Scarola's *SS*
121 Church Av
(bet. E 2 St &
McDonald Av)
435-8800
• Good, homemade
Italian food and
tremendous
portions. **122**C

Seasons *SS*
556 Driggs Av
(bet. N 7 & 8 Sts)
384-9695 (M) (CO)
• American bistro in
Williamsburg. **104**B

Senegal *SS*
1438 Flatbush Av
(bet. Farragut &
Glenwood Rds)
• Dine on the tradi-
tional Haitian tassot
(grilled goat)
and dance the night
away at this restau-
rant/ nightclub. **129**A

Sette Colli *SS*
476 Bay Ridge Av
(bet. Fourth & Fifth
Avs) 921-0909
• Romantic setting,
unobtrusive service
and great Italian
food. **126**B

Short Ribs *S*
9101 Third Av
@ 91 St, 745-0614
Fun place to
pig out with a
raucous, barn
dance feel. **115**

Siam Garden *S*
172 Court St
(bet. Amity &
Congress Sts)
596-3300
• Typical, tasty
Thai in an exotic
space. **107**

Stylowa *S*
694 Manhattan Av
(bet. Nassau &
Norman Avs)
383-8993 (CO)
• Homemade Polish
food in Greenpoint
102

**Sugarhill
Restaurant &
Supper Club** *S*
609 DeKalb Av
@ Nostrand Av
797-1727
• Classic country
cooking with an
urbane flair. **110**

Sunma *S*
5918 Eighth Av
(bet. 60 & 61 Sts)
439-4502 (CO)
• Cozy restaurant
specializing in
fresh Malaysian
cuisine. **127**

ur Restaurant *$*
32 Smith St
bet. Douglas &
utler Sts)
75-1716 (M)
• *Argentine fare.
Saturday and
Sunday Brunch.*
107C

ybil's *$*
210 Church Av
@ Flatbush Av
69-9049 (CO)
• *West Indian bak-
ry and restaurant.*
122B

aeng Fong *$*
504-06 Bay Pkwy
bet. 65 & 66 Sts)
36-9565
• *Traditional
Chinese menu with
reat curries.* **127**D

amarind Tree *$*
463 Flatbush Av
@ Glenwood Road
34-9610 (CO)
• *Tropical paradise
xcelling in flavorful
Caribbean
uisine.* **129**A

eddy's Bar & Grill
96 Berry St
@ N 8 St
84-9787 (CO)
• *Simple pub food at
his young artist
angout in
Williamsburg.*
102C

Teresa's *$*
80 Montague St
(bet. Henry & Hicks
Sts) 797-3696 (CO)
• *Hearty Polish fare.*
108C

Thai Café *$*
925 Manhattan Av
@ Kent Av
383-3562 (CO)
• *Great inexpensive
Thai food.* **102**D

Thristino's *$$*
9703 Third Av
(bet. Marine Av &
97 St) 238-8781 (SM)
• *Italian and American
cuisine in an art
deco interior.* **126**C

T. J. Bentley's *$$*
7110 Third Av
(bet. 71 & 72 Sts)
745-0748 (M)
• *Great supper club
with solid food.* **126**B

**Tokyo of
Brooklyn** *$$*
2954 Av U (bet. E 29
St & Nostrand Av)
891-6221
• *Glatt kosher
sushi.* **137**D

Tommaso's *$$*
1464 86 St
(bet. 14 & 15 Avs)
236-9883
• *Consistent Italian
food in a beautiful,
dimly lit room.* **135**A

Topaze *$*
1875 Utica Av
@ Flatlands
444-7070 (CO)
• *Jamaican eatery
with a full range
of West Indian
cuisine.* **130**C

Tripoli *$$*
156 Atlantic Av
@ Clinton St
596-5800
• *Fabulous Middle
Eastern cuisine in
an elegant and
imaginative
setting.* **107**C

Tuscany Grill *$$*
8620 Third Av
(bet. 86 & 87 Sts)
921-5633
• *Traditional Tuscan
menu including
pizza.* **126**C

Tutta Pasta *$*
160 Seventh Av
(bet. Garfield St &
First Pl)
788-9500
• *Basic and simple
is the theme at
this small Italian
restaurant.* **115**C

**Twelfth St Bar
and Grill** *$$*
1123 Eighth Av
@ 12 St
965-9526
• *American cuisine
in a contemporary
setting with cozy
furnishings.* **115**C

Two Boots *$*
514 Second St
(bet. Seventh &
Eighth Avs)
499-3253
• *Cajun–Italian
cuisine that pairs
the culinary boots
of Louisiana and
Italy.* **115**C

Two Steps Down *$$*
240 DeKalb Av
(bet. Vanderbilt
& Clermont Avs)
399-2020
• *Charming Fort
Greene bistro with
a homey feeling and
a menu full of daily
specials.* **110**C

Two Toms *$*
255 Third Av
@ Union St
875-8689 (SM) (CO)
• *Lack of atmos-
phere becomes the
atmosphere at this
quirky Italian
retreat.* **115**A

Uncle Pho *$$*
263 Smith St
(bet. Douglas &
Degraw Sts)
855-8709
• *Fabulous Asian-
American fusion
cuisine served with
finesse in a bright
space.* **114**B

Vera Cruz *$*
95 Bedford Av
(bet. 6 & 7 Sts)
383-3562
• *Hip Mexican joint
featuring a sidewalk
bar and cozy back
garden.* **104**B

Villa Paradiso *$$*
1969 Bath Av
(bet. 19 & 20 Avs)
837-2696
• *Relaxing
Italian dining
experience.* **135**D

Villa Ruggiero *$$*
2274 86th St
(bet. 22 & 23 Avs)
373-2590 (M)
• *Traditional Italian
fare with an old
world flair.* **135**D

**Waterfront Ale
House** *$$*
155 Atlantic Av
(bet. Clinton &
Henry Sts)
522-3794
• *Micro–brewed
beers and amazing-
ly good food.* **107**C

BROOKLYN EATS

For detailed reviews
of Brooklyn's Best
restaurants,
pick-up a copy of
"Brooklyn Eats"
at your local
bookstore

PRICE KEY

Prices given
include average
cost of a dinner
and an alcoholic
beverage without
tax and tip.

$ = $5-$20
$$ = $21-$35
$$$ = $36-$55
$$$$ = Over $55

ENTERTAINMENT

BARS & CLUBS

Bar One
9218 Fourth Av
@ 92 St, 745-0777
• Sports bar. **126D**

Club Rio
9235 Fourth Av @ 93
St, 238-6566
• Latin music and
dancing on Friday
and Saturday
nights. Proper attire
required. **126D**

Enigma Nite Club
1546 62 St @ 15 Av
837-8990
• Ladies free on
Latin Wednesday
until 10:30 pm.
Casual but proper
attire. **127D**

Farrell's Bar
277 Prospect Park W
788-8779
• One of the last
bastions of male
dominance. **114C**

**Galapagos
Performance Art
Space**
70 N 6 St (bet.
Wythe & Kent Avs)
782-5188
•Beer and wine bar.
Sushi, live music
and DJ's nightly.
Call for music, the-
ater and art sched-
ule. **102C**

Griswolds Pub
7726 Third Av @ 78
St, 745-3340
• Sunday brunch.
Live music. **126B**

**Hennessy's
Bar & Grill**
442-46 Court St
625-5255
• Brunch, burgers
and beer. **114B**

Legacy Nite Club
437 88 St
(bet. Fourth & Fifth
Avs) 748-1002
•Valet parking.**126D**

Lily's Public House
8814 Third Av
(bet. 88 & 89 Sts)
833-6466
• Sunday brunch.
126C

**NY Coffee House
Exchange Cafe**
7716 Third Av (bet.
77 & 78 Sts)
833-9321
• Modern day cof-
fee house. Live gui-
tar music on Friday.
126B

Odessa
1113 Brighton Beach
Av (bet. Brighton 13
& 14) 332-3223
• A place where
food is plentiful and
the vodka flows
freely. **144D**

Oscars–Golden Gate
3867 Shore Pkwy
@ Knapp St
891-1442
• Live entertainment
Friday and Saturday.
Free parking. **144A**

Paragraph Font
351 Flatbush Av
398-5413
• Call for reserva-
tions and show
times. **107D**

Peggy O'Neill's
8123 Fifth Av
(81 & 82 Sts)
748-1400
Casual attire. **126D**

Pips Comedy Club
2005 Emmons Av
(Ocean Av & E 21
St) 646-9433
• Top comedy
shows Friday and
Saturday. **144B**

**Rasputin
Supper Club**
2670 Coney Island Av
@ Av X)
332-8111 (R)
• French-Russian
dinner, dancing and
flashy floor show.
144A

Rising Cafe
188 Fifth Av
789-6340
• Live traditional
Irish music. **115A**

Rock-N-Jocks
9022 Fourth Av
921-7279
• Sports bar with
22 TVs. DJ on Friday
and Saturday nights.
126D

Ryan's Ale House
8625 Fourth Av
@ 87 St, 836-8524
• Live music or DJ
Thursday thru
Sunday. **126D**

Shortribs
9101 Third Av
745-0614 (MT)
• Live bands and
Sunday brunch.
Proper attire
required. **126C**

Smith's Bar & Grill
440 Fifth Av
(bet. 8 & 9 Sts)
788-9363
• All major sporting
events live via
satellite on 8- foot
screen. 15 beers on
tap. **115C**

**Sugar Hill
Disco & Restaurant**
609 Dekalb Av
797-1727
• Dining, dancing
with live jazz and
blues and other
entertainment. **107D**

**200 Fifth
Restaurant & Bar**
200 Fifth Av
638-2925
• Comedy on
Monday, salsa,
rhythm & blues on
Friday. 23 imports
on tap. **115**

Vybes
238 Flatbush Av
@ Seventh Av
789-0769 **115**

**Waterfront
Ale House**
155 Atlantic Av
(bet. Henry & Clinto
St.) 522-3794
• Great music, burg-
ers and beer. **108**

Wicked Monk
8415 Fifth Av
(bet. 84 & 85 Sts)
921-0601
• 19th century
Irish monastery
decor. **126**

FILM

BAMcinema
30 Lafayette Av
636-4100 **107**

**Brooklyn Heights
Cinemas, Inc.**
70 Henry St
@ Orange St
596-7070 **107**

Canarsie Theater
9310 Av L @ E 93 St
251-0700 **124D**

Cineplex Alpine
6817 Fifth Av
(bet. 68 & 69 St)
777-FILM
+ code 580 **126B**

Cineplex Fortway
6720 Ft Hamilton
Pkwy (bet. 67
& 68 Sts)
777-FILM + code 578
or 238-4200 **127A**

**Cineplex
Kenmore Quad**
1101 Church Av
(off Flatbush Av)
777-FILM
+ code 576 **122B**

**Cineplex
Kings Plaza**
Kings Plaza Mall
Upper Level
(Flatbush Av & Av U)
777-FILM + code 579
or 253-1110 **138B**

**Cineplex
Kingsway Fiveplex**
946 Kings Hwy
@ Coney Island Av
777-FILM + code 577
or 645-8588 **136B**

Cobble Hill Cinema
265 Court St
596-9113 **114B**

**Commodore
Theater**
329 Broadway
(near Marcy Av)
384-7259 **104D**

Kent Triplex
1168 Coney Island
Av @ Av I
338-3371 **136D**

Ocularis Films
70 N 6 St (bet. Wythe
& Kent Avs)
388-8713
• BYOB to this con-
verted mayonnaise
factory. Call for
schedule of indepen-
dent, cult and classic
films. **102C**

**The Pavilion Movie
Theatres**
188 Prospect Park W
369-0838
• Restored
multiplex theater
complete with a
cafe. **115C**

Plaza Twin Cinema
314 Flatbush Av
@ Seventh Av
636-0170 **115B**

UA Marlboro
6817 Bay Pkwy
@ 69 St
232-4000 **127A**

**UA @
Sheepshead Bay**
3907 Shore Pkwy
(Harkness Av &
Knapp St) 615-1700
Parking. **146A**

MUSIC &
THEATRE

Arts at St. Ann's
157 Montague St
@ Clinton St
834-8794
• Host to a calendar
of classical music,
jazz, blues, opera,
dance and
theater. **108D**

Bargemusic Ltd.
Fulton Ferry Landing
624-4061
• A year-round pro-
gram of chamber
music on a floating
concert hall. **107A**

**Billie Holiday
Theatre**
1368 Fulton St
@ New York Av
857-6363
• Outstanding
new plays and
musicals. **116B**

**Brooklyn Academy
of Music (BAM)**
30 Lafayette Av
@ Ashland Pl
636-4100
• America's oldest
performing arts
center, with four
performance spaces
that offer imagina-
tive and innovative
events including
music, dance and
drama. **107D**

**BAM
Harvey Theatre**
Fulton St
@ Rockwell Pl
636-4100
• Music, dance,
drama at this BAM
venue. **107D**

**Brooklyn Center for
the Performing Arts
at Brooklyn College
(BCBC)** Campus Rd
@ Hillel Pl
951-4500
• World class venue
presenting interna-
tionally acclaimed
artists. **129A**

**Brooklyn
Philharmonic
Orchestra**
30 Lafayette Av
@ Ashland Pl
636-4137 **129A**
• Innovative orches-
tra performing at
BAM and special
events across
Brooklyn. **107D**

**Brooklyn
Youth Chorus**
138 Court St
243-9447
• Nationally known
chorus provides
concerts through-
out Brooklyn. **129A**

**Celebrate
Brooklyn!**
855-7882
• Summer festival at
Prospect Park

Bandshell. **129A**

**Gowanus Arts
Exchange**
421 5 Av @ 8 St
832-0018
• Produces a varied
family program of
dance, theater,
performance art
and music year–
round. **115A**

The Puppet Works
338 Sixth Av
965-3391
• Dedicated to the
preservation and
presentation of tra-
ditional marionette
theatre. **115C**

651, An Arts Center
651 Fulton St
636-4181
• Culturally diverse
arts programs
at the award–
winning Majestic
Theater. **107D**

**Thelma Hill
Performing Arts
Center**
30 Third Av–Rm 602
875-9710
• Features works
of up and coming
artists and dance
ensembles. **107D**

ENTERTAINMENT

EDUCATION

COLLEGES & UNIVERSITIES

Boricua College
186 North 6 St
782-2200 **104A**

Brooklyn College
2900 Bedford Av
951-5671 **129A**

Brooklyn Law School
250 Joralemon St
625-2200 **108D**

Kingsborough Community College
2001 Oriental Bd
368-5000 **145C**

Long Island University
1 University Plz
488-1011 **109C**

Medgar Evers College (CUNY)
1150 Carroll St
270-6022 **116C**

New York City Technical College
300 Jay St
260-5000 **108B**

Polytechnic University
5 MetroTech Center
260-3500 **109C**

Pratt Institute
200 Willoughby Av
636-36468 **110D**

St. Francis College
180 Remsen St
522-2300 **108D**

St. Joseph's College
245 Clinton Av
636-6800 **110C**

Cush Campus
221 Kingston Av
756-0333 **116B**

HIGH SCHOOLS

Bishop Kearney
2202 69 St
236-6363 **126D**

Bishop Ford
500 19 St
965-6400 **121B**

Bishop Laughlin
357 Clermont Av
857-2700 **110C**

Boys & Girls
1700 Fulton St
467-1700 **117A**

Brooklyn Friends School
375 Pearl St
852-1029 **108D**

Brooklyn Technical
DeKalb Av
@ Ft Greene Pl
858-5150 **109D**

Edward R Murrow
1600 Av L
258-9283 **128D**

El Puente Academy
211 S 4 St
599-2895 **104A**

Fort Hamilton
8301 Shore Rd
748-1537 **126C**

John Dewey
50 Av X
373-6400 **137D**

George Westinghouse
105 Johnson St
858-8334 **109A**

High School of Telecommunications, Arts & Technology
6700 Fourth Av
745-4800 **126B**

Midwood
Bedford Av &
Glenwood Rd
859-9200 **129A**

Packer Collegiate
170 Joralemon St
875-6644 **108D**

Poly Prep CDS
9216 Seventh Av
836-9800 **134B**

St. Ann's School
129 Pierrepont St
@ Clinton St
522-1660 **108D**

St. Joseph's
80 Willoughby St
624-3618 **109C**

Xaverian
7100 Shore Rd
836-7100 **126A**

LEARNING CENTERS

ASA Institute of Business & Computer Technology
151 Lawrence St
522-9073 **109C**

Career Training Center
175 Remsen St
855-5454 **108D**

F.E.G.S. Trades & Business School
199 Jay St, 3 flr
488-0120 **108D**

Institute of Design and Construction
141 Willoughby St
855-3661 **109C**

Kaplan Educational Center
1602 Kings Hwy
336-5300 **137A**

Maritime Workshop
Brooklyn Navy Yard
Berth 11–Captain's
Boathouse
260-8965 **107B**

MetroTech Career Institute
384 Atlantic Av
855-7060 **107C**

National Vocational School
5922 20 Av
256-3233 **128C**

LIBRARIES

Brooklyn Business Library
280 Cadman Plz W
722-3333 **108**

The Brooklyn Historical Society
128 Pierrepont St
624-0890 **108**

Brooklyn Public Library
Grand Army Plz
780-7700 **115**

The Kurdish Library Museum
144 Underhill Av
783-7930 **115**

SPECIAL LEARNING

Avalon Academy
695-705 Sixth Av
768-4300 **121**

Helen Keller Services for the Blind
57 Willoughby St
522-2122 **109**

Mary McDowell Center for Learning
110 Schermerhorn
625-3939 **107**

St. Francis de Sales School for the Deaf
260 Eastern Pkwy
636-4573 **116**

YAI
460 W 34 St, MA
212-563-7474

BOROUGH & CITY HALL

Borough Hall
Office of the
Borough President
209 Joralemon St
802-3700 **108D**

City Hall, MA
• City Council
212-788-7100
• Mayor's Office
212-788-3000

EMERGENCY & ENFORCEMENT

Call 911—
when it's a matter
of life or death.
All other emergency
calls (heat, water,
gas and power)
should be directed
to appropriate city
agencies and
utilities.

Fire Dept Hdqrs
9 MetroTech Center
718-694-2000 **109C**

**Police Dept Hdqrs
& Central Booking**
120 Schermerhorn St
718-875-6586 **108D**

60th Police Precinct
2951 W 8 St
946-3311 **136D**

61st Police Precinct
2575 Coney Island Av
627-6611 **137C**

62nd Police Precinct
1925 Bath Av
236-2611 **135D**

63rd Police Precinct
1844 Brooklyn Av
258-4411 **116D**

66th Police Precinct
5822 16 Av
851-5611 **127D**

67th Police Precinct
2820 Snyder Av
287-3211 **123A**

68th Police Precinct
333 65 St
439-4211 **120D**

69th Police Precinct
9720 Foster Av
257-6211 **124B**

70th Police Precinct
154 Lawrence Av
851-5511 **128C**

71st Police Precinct
421 Empire Bd
735-0511 **116D**

72nd Police Precinct
830 Fourth Av
935-6311 **114D**

73rd Police Precinct
1470 East New York
Av 495-5411 **117B**

75th Police Precinct
1000 Sutter Av
827-3511 **119A**

76th Police Precinct
191 Union St
834-3211 **114B**

77th Police Precinct
127 Utica Av
735-0611 **117A**

78th Police Precinct
65 Sixth Av
636-6411 **115B**

79th Police Precinct
263 Tompkins Av
636-6611 **111C**

81st Police Precinct
30 Ralph Av
574-0411 **111D**

83rd Police Precinct
480 Knickerbocker
Av 574-1605 **112A**

84th Police Precinct
301 Gold St
875-6811 **109A**

88th Police Precinct
298 Classon Av
636-6511 **110D**

90th Police Precinct
211 Union Av
963-5311 **114B**

94th Police Precinct
100 Messerole Av
383-3879 **102D**

US Coast Guard
Floyd Bennett Field
615-2400 **439D**

JUSTICE

The State & City
court system is
undergoing a major
overhaul in the year
2000. Here is a short
key to the jurisdic-
tions of the current
system.

• Civil— for disputes
under $25,000
• Criminal— for
misdemeaners
• Family— for child
custody issues
• Surrogate— for
probation of wills
• Supreme— civil
cases over $25,000,
divorce and felonies.

County Clerk
360 Adams St
643-5897 **108D**

Supreme Court 2
Johnson St
643-8076 **108D**

**District
Attorney's Office**
210 Joralemon St
250-2000 **108D**

Civil
141 Livingston St
212-791-6000 **108D**

Criminal
120 Schermerhorn St
643-4044 **108D**

Family
283 Adams St
643-265 **108D**

Supreme–Kings Co
360 Adams St
643-8076 **108D**

Surrogate's
2 Johnson St
643-5262 **108D**

Small Claims (Civil)
141 Livingston St
108D

SOCIAL & CIVIL SERVICES

**NYC Board
of Education**
110 Livingston St
935-4259 **108D**

**NYC Board
of Elections**
345 Adams St
330-2250 **108D**

Dept. of Finance
345 Adams St **108D**

**NYC Human
Resources
Administration–
Child Welfare**
345 Adams St **108D**

NYS Dept. of Labor
115 Lawrence St
109C

**Marriage
License Bureau**
Municipal Building
802-3581 **108D**

**Subway & Bus
Transit Information**
330-1234

GOVERNMENT

HEALTHCARE

HOSPITALS

Beth Israel Medical Center–Kings Highway Division
3201 Kings Hwy
(bet. E 32 St & New York Av)
252-3000   **129D**

The Brookdale University Hospital and Medical Center
One Brookdale Plz
@ Linden Bd
240-5000   **124A**

Brooklyn Hospital Center–
• Downtown Center
121 DeKalb Av
@ Ashland Pl
250-8000   **109D**
• Caledonian Center
100 Parkside Av
@ St. Paul's Pl
250-8000   **122A**

Coney Island Hospital
2601 Ocean Pkwy
@ Shore Pkwy
616-3000   **144A**

Interfaith Medical Center
555 Prospect Pl
@ Classon Av
935-7007   **116A**

Interfaith Medical Center–St. John's Episcopal Site
1545 Atlantic Av
@ Herkimer Pl
604-6000   **117A**

King's County Hospital Center
451 Clarkson Av
(bet. New York and Brooklyn Avs)
245-3901   **123A**

Kingsbrook Jewish Medical Center
585 Schenectady Av
604-5000   **123B**

Long Island College Hospital (LICH)
339 Hicks St
@ Atlantic Av
780-1000   **108C**

Lutheran Medical Center
150 55 St @ Second Av, 630-7000   **120D**

Maimonides Medical Center
4802 Tenth Av
(bet. 48 & 49 Sts)
283-6000   **121C**

NY Community Hospital
2525 Kings Hwy
692-5300   **137A**

NY Methodist Hospital
506 Sixth St (bet. Seventh and Eighth Avs) 780-3000   **115C**

St. Mary's Hospital of Brooklyn
170 Buffalo Av
@ Rochester Av
221-3000   **117A**

State University of New York Health Science Center at Brooklyn (SUNY Downstate Hospital)
470 Clarkson Av
(bet. New York and Brooklyn Avs)
270-1000   **123A**

Staten Island University Hospital
475 Seaview Av, SI
226-2500

Veterans Administration Hospital
800 Poly Pl
836-6600   **134B**

Victory Memorial Hospital
9036 Seventh Av
567-1234   **134B**

Woodhull Medical and Mental Health Center
760 Broadway
963-8000   **105C**

Wyckoff Heights Medical Center
374 Stockholm St
963-7735   **105D**

MEDICAL CENTERS & HOMES

Ambulatory Surgery Center of Brooklyn
313 43 St
369-1900   **121A**

Augustana Lutheran Home
5434 Second Av
630-6000   **120D**

Bay Park Medical, P.C.
794 Union St
636-0335   **115A**

Bedford Stuyvesant Family Health Center, Inc.
1413 Fulton St
636-4500   **116B**

Brooklyn Center for Psychotherapy
300 Flatbush Av
@ Seventh Av
622-2000   **115B**

Brooklyn Psychiatric Center, Inc.
189 Montague St
875-7510   **108D**

Brooklyn Women's Services, LLC (Affiliated with Maimonides Medical Center)
9201 Fourth Av
748-1234   **126D**

Cancer Institute of Brooklyn at Maimonides Medical Center
6323 Seventh Av
283-6956   **127A**

CNR Health Care Network, Inc.
520 Prospect Pl
636-1000   **116A**

Cobble Hill Health Center
380 Henry St
855-6789   **106B**

Cumberland Diagnostic & Treatment Center
100 N Portland Av
260-7531   **109B**

Downtown Integrated Medical Services, P.C.
81 Willoughby St
(bet. Lawrence and Bridge Sts)
522-3399   **109C**

Girling Health Care, Inc.
9410 Flatlands Av
@ 95 St
485-9301   **124D**

Greenpoint Medical Care
66 Nassau Av
(bet. Manhattan Av & Lorimer St)
383-4600.   **102D**

Healthsouth Physical Therapy
5402 Av N
252-0300   **130C**

Maimonides Medical Center– Boro Park Primary Care
1002 49 St
437-5000   **127B**

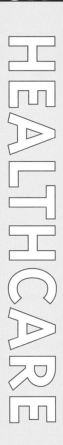

Maimonides Medical Center–Brooklyn Family Medical Associates
8210 18 Av
331-6600 **135B**

Maimonides Medical Center–Cancer Institute of Brooklyn
701 64 St
283-8587 **127A**

Maimonides Medical Center–Cardiac Institute
4802 Tenth Av
(bet. 48 & 49 Sts)
283-8902 **127B**

Maimonides Children's Services
• 8212 18 Av @ 82 St
331-3939 **135B**
• 1301 57 St
(bet. 13 and 14 Avs)
283-7600 **127B**
• 5301 Eighth Av
(bet. 53 & 54 Sts)
633-0300 **121C**

Marcus Garvey Nursing Home
810 St. Marks Av
(bet. New York and Brooklyn Avs)
467-7300 **116B**

Metropolitan Jewish Geriatric Center
4914 Fort Hamilton
Pkwy @ Tenth Av
851-5978 **127B**

NY Congregational Nursing Center
135 Linden Bd
(bet. Bedford & Rogers Avs)
693-6060 **122B**

NY Methodist Hospital–Faculty Practice
263 Seventh Av
246-8500 **115A**

NY Methodist Hospital–South Brooklyn Health Center
120 Richards St
834-8202 **114A**

NY Methodist Hospital–Family Health Centers
• 1910 Nostrand Av
284-4440 **123C**
• 210 Flatbush Av
783-0070 **107D**
• 5923 16 Av
259-6122 **122B**
• 894 Manhattan Av
383-3377 **102D**

NY Methodist Hospital–Bay Ridge Diagnostic Center & Treatment Services
6740 Third Av
921-0206 **126B**

NY Methodist Hospital–Medical Associates
1301 Avenue J
677-0101 **128D**

NYU Medical Offices
1 Prospect Park W
230-4260 **115D**

Palm Gardens Nursing Home
615 Av C
633-3300 **122C**

River Manor Care Center
630 East 104 St
272-1050 **124B**

Spinecare
3500 Nostrand Av
769-2521 **137D**

St. Mary's Hospital of Brooklyn–Charles Drew Family Health Center
342 Kingsboro
Third Wk
778-1003 **117A**

St. Mary's Hospital of Brooklyn–St. Francis of Assisi Family Health Center
333 Knickerbocker
Av, 381-5600 **112A**

St. Mary's Hospital of Brooklyn–Sister Lucian Lucchi Family Health Center
160 Menahan St
455-5400 **108D**

St. Mary's Hospital of Brooklyn–St. Peter Claver Family Health Center
1061 Liberty Av
827-5009 **119A**

St. Mary's Hospital of Brooklyn–Sister Thea Bowman Family Health Center
1205 Sutter Av
953-6006 **119B**

University Hospice of Staten Island University Hospital
256 Mason Av, SI
226-6450

Willoughby Nursing Home
949 Willoughby Av
443-1600 **109C**

HOLISTIC CENTERS

Brooklyn Medical Center for Holistic Health
2176 Nostrand Av
(bet. Av H & Flatbush Av)
859-3222 **129D**

The Exercise Studio
7 Bay 28 St
998-3694 **135D**

Feldenkrais Center of Cobble Hill
418 Henry St
875-9348 **108C**

PHARMACIES

Genovese (24hr)
2064 Mill Av
531-0408 **130D**

Neergaard Pharmacies (24hr)
454 Fifth Av @ 9 St
768-0600 **115C**

Park Ridge Pharmacy
7426 15 Av
331-9099
Open
until 11pm. **127C**

Rite Aid (24hr)
• Bay Ridge
6900 Fourth Av
748-8184 **126B**
• Gravesend
185 Kings Hwy
837-6531 **136A**

Thriftway Kings Pharmacy (24hr)
2472 Flatbush Av
(1 block from Kings
Plz) 253-0200 **138B**

Thriftway Pharmacy
1950 Ralph Av
763-5599
Open
until 11pm. **130D**

TO FIND A CENTER

Simply turn to page and locate hospital, medical center or pharmacy in grids A,B,C or D.

KIDS' STUFF

ACTIVITIES

Aquarium for Wildlife Conservation
W 8 St & Surf Av
265-FISH
• Over 10,000 specimens of sea life in natural settings. Incredible dolphin and seal shows. **143C**

Astroland Amusement Park
1000 Surf Av
265-2100
• Premier amusement park. Home of the world famous Cyclone. **143C**

The Brooklyn Children's Museum
145 Brooklyn Av
435-4400
• World's first museum created expressly for children. **116B**

Coney Island Amusement Area
• World famous center of rides, amusements and food. Includes Astroland, The Wonder Wheel, The Cyclone, and Nathan's Famous. Lots to do along the Boardwalk. **143C**

Deno's Wonder Wheel Park
Boardwalk
@ West 12 St
372-2592
• 18 kiddy rides and five major thrill rides including the landmarked Wonder Wheel. **143C**

Discovery Zone FunCenter
5100 Kings Plaza
252-1717
• Laser tag, ball room, mazes, karaoke and other exciting activities for kids of all ages. (supervised) **115D**

FunTime USA
2461 Knapp St
368-0500
• NYC's largest indoor family entertainment center. 55,000 square feet full of activities for children off all ages: arts and crafts, a high–tech video arcade, a three story soft play area and a food court. **137D**

Kate Wollman Rink
Prospect Park
287-6431
• Outdoor ice skating rink. Skate rentals are available. **115D**

Kids N' Action
1149 McDonald Av (between Avs I & J)
377-1818
• Children's activity center for ages one through fourteen. Ideal for birthday parties. **128D**

Nellie Bly Amusement Park
1824 Shore Pkwy
996-4002
• Kiddy rides, attractions, special events, and shows. Birthday parties available. **143C**

The New York Transit Museum
Boerum Pl
@ Schermerhorn St
243-8601, 694-5102
• Explore a 1930s subway station turned museum. This underground adventure showcases vintage railway cars and transit exhibitions. **108D**

Prospect Park
95 Prospect Park W & 4 St, 965-8999
• A 526–acre urban park with historic carousel, skating pond, ball fields, tennis courts, fishing and playgrounds. **115D**

Prospect Park Wildlife Center
450 Flatbush Av
718 399-7339
• State-of-the-art zoo that features seals, red pandas, prairie dogs. **115D**

The Puppetworks
338 Sixth Av
965-3391
• Dedicated to the preservation and presentation of traditional marionette theater. **115C**

The Rotunda Gallery
33 Clinton St
875-4047
• Works by Brooklyn artists and arts education for children. **108B**

Sunset Park
44 St @ Sixth Av.
• Highest point in Brooklyn. Views of Lady Liberty, and the Manhattan skyline. **121C**

SWEET TREATS

Anapoli
6920 Third Av
748-3863
• The old-fashioned kind. **120D**

Once Upon a Sundae
7702 Third Av
748-3412
• Like they did it in the old days. **126D**

Hinschs Confectionery
8518 Fifth Av
748-2854
• Old fashioned ice cream shop. **126D**

Peter's Ice Cream
185 Atlantic Av
852-3835
• Gourmet ice cream, desserts, coffee and outstanding pies. **107C**

Philip's Confections
1237 Surf Av
372-8783
• Famous for over 60 years, this sweet shop carries cotton candy, popcorn, jelly and caramel apples. **143C**

The Scoop, Stop II
263 Prospect Park W
788-0524 **115D**

Seebodes
4920 Fifth Av
@ 50 St
748-9375
• Handmade candies! **120D**

Taste of the Tropics Ice Cream
1249 Utica Av
@ Av D
629-3582
• Flavors like mango, papaya and rum raison are a few of their 30 delicious flavors. **123D**

LODGING

SWIMMING POOLS

Indoor

Brownsville Center
555 Linden Bd
345-2706   **123**A

St. John's Center
1251 Prospect Pl
771-2787   **115**B

Mini Pools

**American
Playground**
Franklin & Milton
Sts, 349-7904   **102**B

David Fox Park
East 54 St & Av H
331-2437   **130**A

Glenwood Houses
Farragut Road &
Ralph Av
531-2480   **124**C

HS 57
117 Stuyvesant Av
452-0519   **111**D

Windower Park
60 St & Mill Av
349-7904   **130**D

IS 20
Adelphia & Clemont
Av, 625-6101   **107**D

IS 44
Madison & Monroe
St, 919-2582   **111**C

Sunset Park Library
4 St & Fourth Av
    120D

Outdoor

Betsy Head
Livonia & Dumont
Avs 965-6581   **117**D

Bushwick Center
Flushing Av &
Humbolt St
452-2116   **105**C

**Commodore
Barry Center**
Flushing Av
@ N Elliot St,
243-2593   **109**A

Douglas Center
Degraw St
(bet. Third Av
@ Nevins St)
625-3268   **115**A

Howard Center
Howard Av
(bet. Glenmore &
East New York Av)
385-1023   **117**D

Kosciusko Center
Kosciusko (bet.
Marcy & DeKalb Av)
622-5271   **111**C

Red Hook Center
Corner of Bay &
Henry Sts
722-3211   **114**D

Sunset Center
Seventh Av & 43 St
965-6578   **121**C

LODGINGS

Akwaaba Mansion
347 McDonough St
455-5958
• *Akwaaba is the
Ghana word for
welcome. Four
guest rooms with
mixed African and
Victorian Decor.*
    117A

**Baisley House
Bed & Breakfast**
935-1959
• *Restored 19th
century Victorian
brownstone in
historic district of
Carroll Gardens.*

**Bed & Breakfast
On The Park**
499-6115
• *Restored Victorian
brownstone on
Prospect Park.*

**Comfort Inn
Brooklyn**
8315 Fourth Av
800-447-3467
• *Newly renovated
70–room hotel in
Bay Ridge.*   **126**D

**Four Points
Sheraton Hotel
JFK Airport**
151-20 Baisley Bd,
QS, 489-1000
• *Luxurious four–
star hotel with 185
rooms. An oasis
near JFK Airport.*

**Foy House
Bed & Breakfast**
636-1492
819 Carroll St
• *Brooklyn's oldest
bed and breakfast
located in Park
Slope.*   **115**D

**Golden Gate
Motor Inn**
3867 Shore Pkwy
743-4000
• *150–room hotel
in Sheepshead
Bay.*   **145**A

**Holiday Inn
at JFK Airport**
144-02 135 Av
Jamaica, QS
659-0200
• *360–room, ten–
year–old hotel with
many amenities for
world travelers.*

**Homestay
New York**
434-2071
• *Affordable lodging
in fine Brooklyn
homes for interna-
tional tourists.*

**LaGuardia
Marriott Hotel**
102-05 Ditmars Bd
East Elmhurst, QS
565-8900
• *Newly renovated
436–room hotel
near Laguardia
Airport.*

**New York
Marriott Brooklyn**
333 Adams St
246-7000
• *Brooklyn's brand
new luxury hotel
offers 376 rooms
for business
and leisure
travelers.*   **108**D

Park House
1206 48 St
871-8100
• *Apartments for
rent with kitch-
enette for short
term stays in Boro
Park.*   **127**B

**The Staten
Island Hotel**
1415 Richmond Av,
SI, 698-5000
• *187 comfortable
rooms in nearby
Staten Island.*

RESERVATIONS

At Home in NY
800-692-4262

City Lights B & B
212-737-7049

Homestay NY
434-2071.

NY by Phone
888-NYC-APPLE

New World
800-443-3800

Urban Ventures
212-594-5650

SHOPPING

NEIGHBORHOOD SHOPPING STREETS

• *Brooklyn is home to great shopping; check out these streets and neighborhoods!*

Atlantic Avenue
Brooklyn Heights–
Boerum Hill

Avenue J
Midwood

Avenue M
Midwood

Avenue U
Gravesend–
Marine Park

Avenue X
Gravesend

Bay Parkway
Bensonhurst

Brighton Beach Avenue
Brighton Beach

Broadway
Bushwick

Church Avenue
East Flatbush

Columbia Street
Columbia Terrace

Coney Island Avenue
Flatbush

Court Street
Cobble Hill–
Carroll Gardens

De Kalb Avenue
Clinton Hill

Emmons Avenue
Sheepshead Bay

Flatbush Avenue
Downtown
to Mill Basin

Fulton Street
Fort Greene to
Bedford Stuyvesant

Grand Street
Williamsburg

Kings Highway
Midwood

Knickerbocker Avenue
Ridgewood

Lee Avenue
Williamsburg

Liberty Avenue
City Line

Manhattan Avenue
Greenpoint

Montague Street
Brooklyn Heights

Myrtle Avenue
Clinton Hill

New Lots Avenue
East New York

New Utrecht Avenue
Borough Park

Nostrand Avenue
Crown Heights

Pennsylvania Avenue
Starrett City

Ralph Avenue
Georgetown

Rockaway Parkway
Canarsie

Sheepshead Bay Road
Sheepshead Bay

Smith Street
Carroll Gardens

3rd Avenue
Bay Ridge

5th Avenue
Park Slope–
Bay Ridge

7th Avenue
Park Slope

8th Avenue
Sunset Park

13th Avenue
Boro Park

18th Avenue
Bensonhurst

86th Street
Bay Ridge–
Bensonhurst

SHOPPING CENTERS

Atlantic Center
Atlantic Av
(bet. Ft Greene Pl
& S Oxford Pl)
• *Brooklyn's newest Mall with Old Navy, Caldor's, Kids R' Us and Circuit City among others.* **107D**

K-Mart Plaza
Bay Pkwy
@ Shore Pkwy
• *K-Mart, Toys 'R Us and many other stores with parking.* **135D**

Fulton Mall
6 block stretch
on Fulton St
(bet. Adams St/
Boerum Pl and
Flatbush Av)
852-5118
• *Home to 450 stores including Macy's.* **109C**

The Gallery at MetroTech
1 Dekalb Av
(Located on
Fulton Mall)
• *The former Albee Square Mall is now home to Toys 'R Us, a variety of stores and a food court.* **109C**

Kings Plaza
5100 Kings Plz
(Flatbush Av & Av U
253-6842
• *Brooklyn's original mall boasts Sears, Macy's and some of the biggest retail chains among its 150 stores and restaurants. All day parking available for $1.* **138**

SPECIALTY FOODS

Aiello Brother Cheese Company
7609 18 Av
(bet. 76 & 77 St)
256-1151
• *They make and ship 41,000 pounds of mozzarella cheese a week– all made with grade A milk.* **135**

Bari Pork Store
7119 18 Av
837-1257
• *Offers Mozzarella ricotta, bocconcini, stuffed chicken croquettes plus pork sausage filled with smoked mozzarella.* **127**

Charcuterie
244 Flatbush Av
@ St Marks Pl
783-2359
• *Specialty cheese and food items.* **115**

SHOPPING

Eagle Cheese Company
420 Av U
332-7852
  Homemade ravioli, manicotti, mini-pizzas and imported cheeses. **136D**

Eagle Provisions
228 Fifth Av
499-0026
  Polish Maas-hammer, Krinos feta from Greece, pot cheese, and sharp cheddars in ten varieties from England, France, Germany, Italy and New York. **114D**

Europa Pastry Shop
7007 65 St
232-4845
  Custom wedding cakes. **128C**

Famous Kosher Meats
3393 Coney Island Av, 377-3663 **128D**

Fortunato Brothers
289 Manhattan Av (corner Devoe St)
387-2281
  Creamy fresh pastries, artistic wedding cakes, and spumoni. **104B**

Haifa Halal Meat & Supermarket
263 Flatbush Av
783-8329 **122B**

Lassen & Hennigs
114 Montague St
875-6272
  • Gourmet market and delicatessen. **108C**

Leske's Bakery
7612 Fifth Av
680-2323
  • Buttery Danish pastry and Swedish lemp (rye with molasses) bread. **126B**

Lioni Latticini Mozzarella Co.
7819 15 Av
232-7852
  • 15 types of fresh and smoked mozzarella di bufala from Naples. **127C**

Mejlander & Mulgannon
7615 Fifth Av
238-6666
  • Lingonberry jam, flatbreads and other Scandinavian staples. **126B**

Mona Lisa Bakery
1476 86 St
837-9053
  • Third generation Italian bakery. **135A**

Nordic Delicacies
6909 Third Av
748-1874
  • They make their own meatballs and fish pudding daily. **126B**

Park Slope Brewing Company
40 Van Dyke St
246-8050
  • Call to arrange a guided tour of the micro-brewery. **114A**

Peregrine Grocery
50 Henry St
no phone
  • This country store in the city, offers great cheeses and other delights. **108B**

Pollio
398 Fifth Av
768-6887
  • Sumptuous sandwiches and stellar sausages. **115A**

Regina Bakery
256 Prospect Park W
499-0377 **115D**

Sahadi Import Co. Inc.
187-189 Atlantic Av (bet. Clinton & Court St) 624-4550
  • They carry 120 specialty cheeses, Middle Eastern delicacies, olives, hummus, etc. **108D**

Tedone Grocery Store
597 Metropolitan Av
387-5830
  • Family-owned business for 75 years that has great fresh mozzarella. **104B**

Two For the Pot
200 Clinton St (bet. State St & Atlantic Av)
855-8173
  • Coffees, teas and herbs. **108D**

W-Nassau Meat Market
915 Manhattan Av (bet. Kent St. & Greenpoint Av) **102B**

Wedel
Manhattan Av @ Meserole St
no phone
  • Chocolate straight from Poland. **102D**

FESTIVALS & STREET FAIRS

Atlantic Antic
Atlantic Av
Late Sept or Oct
875-8993

Blessing of the Fleet
Sheepshead Bay
3rd week of May
646-9206

Brighton Jubilee
Brighton Beach Av
Sunday before Labor Day
891-0800

DanceAfrica Festival
BAM parking lot
Late May or June
636-4100

Feast of Our Lady of Mt. Carmel & St. Paulinus
Greenpoint
Early July
384-0223

Flatbush Av Bonanza
Bet. Grand Army Plz & Pacific St
Early October
783-1685

Mermaid Parade
Coney Island
Late June
372-5159

Midwood Mardi Gras
Av M in Midwood
June
376-0999

Third Av Festival
Bay Ridge
Sunday in Fall
238-6600

Welcome Back to Brooklyn
Grand Army Plz
2nd Sunday in June
855-7882

West Indian American Day Carnival
Eastern Parkway
Labor Day
625-1515

SPORTS 3

BIKING

Bicycling Paths
• Coney Island Boardwalk, (5 to 10 am, from Memorial to Labor Day) **143C**
• Prospect Park (7a.m. to 10p.m, Ocean Pkwy from Church Av to Sea Breeze Av) **122C**
• Shore Pkwy Path (from Owl's Head Park to Cropsey Av and from Knapp St to JFK) **115D**

BOATING

Prospect Park Lake
(near Lincoln Rd & Parkside Av)
282-7789
• Pedal-boat rental near Wollman Rink. **122A**

Sebago Canoe Club
Paedergat Bay
241-3683
• Oldest canoe club in the city that has a large fleet of kayaks. **131A**

BOWLING

Gil Hodges Lanes
6161 Strickland Av
763-3333 **130D**

Maple Lanes
1570 60 St
331-9000 **127D**

BEACHES

Atlantic Ocean Beachfront
Brighton 15 St
to W 37 St **144D**

Coney Island Beach
946-1350
• Three miles of public beach recently replenished with new sand plus the famous boardwalk. **143D**

Manhattan Beach
Oriental Bd
& Irwin St
946-1373 **145C**

GOLF

Dyker Beach Golf Course
86 St & 7 Av
836-9722
• 18 holes, par 71, 6360 yards. Practice putting green, pro shop, club pro and lessons. Open year–round, weather permitting. **134B**

Marine Park Golf Course
2880 Flatbush Av
338-7113
• 18 hole, par 72, 6866 yard champion course. Open year–round, weather permitting. **138D**

NATURE

Aquarium for Wildlife Conservation
W 8 St & Surf Av
265-FISH
• One of the nation's largest public marine exhibitions. Features over 10,000 specimens of sea life in natural settings including an interactive children's exhibit. **145C**

Birdwatching
• 43 St & waterfront home to 35 different bird species. (March–April) **120B**
• Plumb Beach Best for shorebirds and horseshoe crabs. (May) **145B**
• Prospect Park Spring migration brings over two dozen types of warblers.(May) **115B**

The Brooklyn Botanic Garden
1000 Washington Av
622-4433
• New York City's premier plant kingdom, housing some 12,000 varieties of flora on 52 acres. Features impressive bonsai collection, Aquatic House and three tropical habitats. **116C**

Brooklyn Center for the Urban Environment (BCUE)
The Tennis House at Prospect Park
788-8500
• Nature, architecture and history tours of Brooklyn. **115D**

Fishing
• Prospect Park Lake No license required. **139C**
• Sheepshead Bay Contact the local fishing operators there. **122A**

Nature Walks
800-201-PARK NYC
• Urban Park Rangers offer free tours, educational programs and festivals year round, which highlight the natural and cultural features of Brooklyn's parklands.

Prospect Park Wildlife Center
450 Flatbush Av
399-7339
• State–of–the–art zoo in Prospect Park that features seals, red pandas, prairie dogs and exhibits of black–crowned night herons. **115D**

PARK & PLAYGROUND COURT & FIELD

Asser Levy/ Seaside Park
Ocean Pkwy & Surf Av & W 5 St & Seabreeze Av
• Bandshell, children's playground, sitting area with chess/checkers an soccer. **143**

Bayview Park
Bayview Av
(bet. W 37 St to Sea Gate Av)
• Beach and walkways overlooking Gravesend Bay. **142**

Bensonhurst Park
Bay Pkwy
& 21 St **135**

Betty K. Rappaport Park– Roller Hockey Rink
53 St & Fort Hamilton Pkwy **121**

Bergen Beach Park
Bergen Av **131**

Bocci Courts
• Carroll Park (Smith & Carroll Sts **114**
• Gravesend Park 18–19 Avs & 55–57 Sts **128**

rooklyn Heights romenade
This scenic walk long the water's dge in Brooklyn eights offers a pectacular view f Manhattan. Veather permitting, is possible to see he Verrazano Jarrows Bridge, the tatute of Liberty nd he Brooklyn ridge. **108A**

anarsie Park
eaview Av & emsen Av
Seven ballfields, layground, sitting rea, summer camp nd special events or children on 30-acres. **131A**

harles & Jesse ome Park
3 St & ahill Rd **121D**

olonel larcus Park
v P (bet. Ocean kwy & E 4 St) **136B**

oney Island USA
208 Surf Av W 12 St 72-5159
Displays, perfor- ances, special vents. Open year ound. **143C**

Dreier–Offerman Park
Shore Pkwy (north of Belt Pkwy) and Bay 44 St
• Soccer and base- ball fields, batting cages, golf range and skating. **135C**

Dyker Beach Park
14 Av, Cropsey Av and Shore Pkwy (Belt Pkwy)
• Great view of the Verrazano Narrows Bridge and Gravesend Bay. **134B**

Friends Field
E 4 St, McDonald Av & Av M **128D**

Fort Greene Park
Between DeKalk and Myrtle Avs
• Olmstead designed park with tennis courts and views of the city. **109D**

George Wingate High School Playing Field
Southeast @ corner of Brooklyn Av & Rutland Rd **116D**

Gravesend Park– Dora Vaccaro Playground
18 Av & 56 St **128C**

John Paul Jones Park
Shore Pkwy & Fort Hamilton Pkwy
• Great view of the Verrazano Narrows Bridge. **134A**

John J. Carty Park
Fort Hamilton Pkwy (bet.101 St & 94 St) **134B**

JHS 201 Playground
80–81 St (bet. Eleven & Twelfth Avs) **427C**

Kaiser Park
Neptune Av & W 28 St
• Ballfields, tennis courts, barbecue site, benches and sitting area. **142C**

Leif Ericson Park & Square
Bet. 66–67 Sts & Fourth Av– Fort Hamilton Pkwy **126B**

Leif Ericson Recreation Area
Eighth Av (bet. 65 St & 66 St) **127A**

McKinley Park
Bay Ridge Pkwy (bet. 73 & 78 Sts) **126D**

Nicholas A. Brizzi Playground
43 St & Tenth Av **121C**

Owls Head Park
Shore Pkwy (bet. Colonial Rd & 68 St)
• Sighted on a bluff overlooking the har- bor. **126A**

Prospect Park
95 Prospect Park W @ 4 St, 965-8999
• 526 landscaped acres with historic carousel, skating pond and playgrounds. **115D**

Prospect Park Bandshell
855-7882 ext. 52
• Home to the "Celebrate Brooklyn Festival," it is the venue for music, dance, and theatre every week-end, June through September. **115D**

Russerel Pederson Playground
Colonial Rd (bet. 83 & 85 Sts) **126C**

SKATING

Abe Stark Ice Skating Rink
W 19 St & Coney Island Boardwalk 946-6535 **143C**

Kate Wollman Rink
Prospect Park 287-6431 **115D**

TOURS

Brooklyn Attitude
398-0939
• Bus and walking tours of Brooklyn available in English, French & Italian.

Brooklyn Borough Hall
209 Joralemon St 875-4047
• 1848 Greek Revival building and bor- ough's seat of gov- ernment. Free tours on Tuesdays at 1 p.m. **108D**

Tours of Hasidic Crown Heights
953-5244 or 800-838-TOURS
• A behind–the– scenes tour of reli- gious and cultural sites normally closed to the general public.

Victorian Flatbush House Tour
469-8990
• Held annually on the last Sunday of April. This tour includes the three historic landmark districts of Prospect Park South, Ditmas Park and Albemarle– Kenmore Terrace.

RECREATION

The Brooklyn
Historical Society

Discovers the Past

embracing the people, places and events of importance in Brooklyn's history

Celebrates the Present

presenting innovative educational programming and exhibits that examine Brooklyn's rich heritage

Shapes the Future

connecting the library and museum collections with state-of-the-art technology, cutting-edge interactive exhibits and rewarding educational programming

The Brooklyn Historical Society
2 MetroTech Center, Suite 4200   Brooklyn, NY 11201
Telephone 718.254.9830   Facsimile 718.254.9869

www.keyspanenergy.com

We've earned one of the highest customer satisfaction ratings in New York State. But we're not resting on our laurels. We'll continue to earn your satisfaction and smiles through superior natural gas and electric products and services, and a commitment to the community. We're KeySpan, and we're happy to be a part of your life.

www.keyspanenergy.com

CREDITS

THE MAN

Van Dam is an award–winning graphic designer, cartographer and information architect. He holds several patents in the field of paper engineering and origami map folding.

Van Dam's maps and packaging designs have been honored by the AIGA, the Industrial Design Society of America, the editors of ID Magazine and been featured on national television.

Among Van Dam's clients are American Express, Chase Manhattan Bank, Bertelsmann AG, Forbes, Getty Oil, LACVB, The Marvel Entertainment Group, The Metropolitan Museum of Art, NYCVB, St Martin's Press, Warner Brothers and the Walt Disney Company.

printed in China

Stephan Van Dam, AIGA
Publisher, General Editor
& Creative Dictator

Staff

Cartographic Design
Gerry Krieg, Günter Vollath
& Stephan Van Dam

Editorial
Fred Lafontaine, *Director*

Proof Reading
George Delury, Patrick
Pardo, Ruth Houston

Photography
André Grossmann

Cover
Yang Zhao

Production Management
Kenneth Kern,
Tomasz Tomaszewski,
Desktop Publishing

Marketing & Distribution
Victor A. Garrido, *Director*

Contributing Editors
Ron Dorfman, David
Henderson, Gail Pellett

VanDam, Inc.
The VanDam Bldg.
11 W 20 St, NYC 10011

vox:	212-929-0416
fax:	212-929-0426
toll-free:	1-800-UNFOLDS
e-mail:	stephan@vandam.com
web:	www.vandam.com

SPECIAL THANKS

We would like to thank the following people for their insight, suggestions and help in producing Manhattan@tlas.

Schuyler Chapin,
  *Cultural Affairs
  Commissioner NYC*
Stuart & Elizabeth Ewen
Mike Feller,
  NYC Parks Dept.
Arthur Gelb,
  New York Times
Serge Guilbault,
  UBC
Andrew Heiskell
Mary Holloway,
  ABNY
Nigel Holmes
Alice Hudson,
  NYPL
Jane Jacobs
Richard Kaplan
Robert Macdonald,
  *Museum of the City
  of New York*
Brendan Sexton,
  Times Square Bid
Jane Weisman,
  Green Thumb
Richard Saul Wurman
  The one and only